Bristol Introductions

BERTRAND RUSSELL

THOEMMES

BERTRAND
RUSSELL

John G. Slater

Preface by
Ray Monk
Series Editor
University of Southampton

THOEMMES PRESS

© Thoemmes Press 1994

Published in 1994 by

Thoemmes Press
11 Great George Street
Bristol BS1 5RR
England

ISBN 1 85506 346 8 – Paperback
ISBN 1 85506 347 6 – Hardback

British Library Cataloguing-in-Publication Data
A CIP record for this title is available from the British Library

Printed in England by
Athenaeum Press Ltd.

CONTENTS

PREFACE *by Ray Monk*   vii

INTRODUCTION   xi

1. A SKETCH OF HIS LIFE   1

2. LOGIC AND THE FOUNDATIONS OF MATHEMATICS   15

3. SCIENTIFIC METHOD IN PHILOSOPHY   27

4. THE THEORY OF DESCRIPTIONS: AN EXAMPLE OF HIS METHOD IN USE   41

5. METAPHYSICS: 'THE SKELETON OF THE WORLD'   47

6. EPISTEMOLOGY: 'A MAP OF THE THEORY OF KNOWLEDGE'   61

7. ETHICS: THE GROUND FOR MORAL RULES   71

8. RELIGION: A SCEPTIC'S TESTAMENT   87

9. POLITICAL THEORY: LIBERAL AND DEMOCRATIC   95

10. POLITICAL ACTIVISM: HIS DUTY TO HIS FAMILY   115

11. THE IMPORTANCE OF THE STUDY OF HISTORY   129

12. THE PROPER ROLE OF EDUCATION
    IN THE LIFE OF THE CHILD   137
13. SOME THOUGHTS ON HIS
    ACHIEVEMENTS   145
BIBLIOGRAPHY OF WORKS CITED OR
MENTIONED   163

PREFACE

John Slater is well known to anyone who has done any original research on the life or the work of Bertrand Russell. A professor of philosophy at Toronto University, he is also an avid book collector, famous for having built up the largest personal collection of Russell's works anywhere in the world. Perhaps unusually among book collectors, Slater actually reads the works in his possession, and his knowledge of Russell's work is generally regarded as approaching omniscience. As well as editing many of the volumes in the superb series of *Collected Papers of Bertrand Russell*, he was also chosen by Routledge to write the introductions for their new series of paperback reprints of some of Russell's most important philosophical works (*The Principles of Mathematics, Our Knowledge of the External World, Introduction to Mathematical Philosophy*, etc.). These introductions are models of lucid assessment and interpretation, revealing Slater to have, like Russell himself, a natural gift for the simple exposition of difficult ideas.

Slater is thus the perfect person to write a general introduction to Russell's work and the present book has been eagerly anticipated for some time. It does not disappoint. Perhaps alone among introductions to Russell's work, it does not confine itself to that small portion of Russell's vast *oeuvre* that has received attention among professional philosophers. Russell published over sixty books and more than two thousand articles. Naturally, these are not all of equal importance: *Principia Mathematica* is one of the most significant contributions to the intellectual history of the twentieth century, while *Satan in the Suburbs* is just an embarrassment; again, 'On Denoting', Russell's famous 1905 article, has had and will continue to have a central place in the philosophical literature, while 'Should Socialists Smoke Good Cigars?', a piece he wrote for an American newspaper in 1932, is, like many such pieces he wrote, merely ephemeral.

The vastness and the diversity of Russell's output presents a problem for anyone setting out to summarize it. What weight should be given to the various parts of this enormous body of work? Among professional philosophers, this problem has generally been solved by treating with the utmost respect Russell's work on logic and mathematics, discussing, though with markedly diminished respect, his epistemology and metaphysics, and finally dismissing in a paragraph or two his writings on ethics, politics, religion and history. The disadvantage of their approach has been that readers of Russell's work have over the years become increasingly selective, so that, by now, Russell is known to many in the profession almost solely as the author of 'On Denoting'. Among such people, *The Principles of Mathematics* and *Principia Mathematica* are unread but respected, while everything else he wrote is both unread and despised. In consequence, a whole generation of philosophers has grown up with little or no knowledge of some of his most interesting philosophical writings, such as *The Analysis of Mind, Our Knowledge of the External World*, and *Human Knowledge*. Meanwhile, outside the academic profession, among ordinary readers, Russell remains a widely admired and well-liked author for the very work that the professionals despise most: his writings on ethics, politics and religion.

John Slater's book provides a useful corrective to the usual academic approach, and, I hope, will do something to help reverse the trend. It is, assuredly, the most wide-ranging short introduction to Russell's work available. For an undergraduate student of philosophy, the most useful chapters will, admittedly, be chapters 2 to 6, in which Slater provides an excellent and admirably clear summary of the work of Russell's that has had the greatest impact upon the development of analytical philosophy – though, even here, his range of citations is considerably greater than that of other commentators. His discussions of Russell's metaphysics and epistemology are, I think, especially good and provide one of the best short summaries available of Russell's work after 1912, which is when conventional accounts of Russell's philosophy usually begin to lose interest.

In his three chapters of Russell's ethics, religious views and political theory, Slater does well to provide some sort of link beteen Russell as a philosopher and Russell as a public figure. Russell's views in these areas were highly publicized during his lifetime and did much to establish his reputation as a philosopher with something to say about important issues in everyday life. As Slater shows, however, Russell was not just reacting to topical questions, but establishing for himself a general, one might almost say philosophical, position of the perennial question of how one should live.

I am, I must confess, rather sceptical about whether Russell's views on the writing of history really deserve a chapter of their own. Certainly, it seems excessive to devote to them as much space as to his work on logic and the foundations of mathematics. Russell as a historian of philosophy is an interesting topic; his *History of Western Philosophy* remains, after all, the most popular single volume work of its kind in print and (despite being the subject of scorn and disapproval among professional historians of philosophy) has had a considerable influence. But, even after reading John Slater on the subject, I remain unconvinced that Russell has much that is original and interesting to say about history generally or that *How to Read and Understand History* is an important work.

This raises my only general qualm about the book. Slater is, I think, generous to a fault in his accounts of Russell's opinions. Russell expressed opinions about such a vast array of subjects that it would be amazing if some of them at least were not utter folly and I would have appreciated rather more indications from Slater as to where, in his view, Russell was being foolish.

Such criticism, however, pales beside the pleasure in having in such an accessible form the benefit of Slater's unrivalled knowledge of Russell's work. It is the best kind of introduction: one that seeks not to replace the work its summarizes but rather to lead people to read it for themselves. It is like a guidebook of a vast and little-explored country. Speaking as a tourist who strayed into this particular country several years ago and has felt lost ever since, I can say with assurance that this is one of the best and most reliable guidebooks available.

Ray Monk
University of Southampton, 1994

INTRODUCTION

This little book is intended as an introduction to Bertrand Russell's life and work, and not, except perhaps incidentally, as an original contribution to Russell studies. Because he lived for nearly a century and wrote for a significant portion of every day for more than sixty of those years, his written work presents a daunting obstacle to anyone seeking to understand him. A short work which discusses a sample of his ideas should therefore prove useful to some who wonder where to begin. It is hoped, of course, that readers of this book will afterwards start their own adventure with Russell. They will find him one of the most stimulating writers of this century and a sheer delight to read.

In 1940 a benighted lawyer in New York City denounced Russell's works as 'lecherous, libidinous, lustful, venerous, erotomaniac, aphrodisiac, irreverent, narrow-minded, untruthful, and bereft of moral fibre', but that lawyer is remembered now only for his silly remarks. Oddly enough, Russell profited from this attack, although it was hardly intended that he should, because the very extravagance of it led to wide publicity and brought him and his books to the notice of many who had never read him. Once they began to read him, the quality of his writing – its wit and its style, its substance and its daring – led them on from book to book. If I can, by a more sympathetic approach, recruit some to share my delight and interest in his work, I shall have reward enough.

Toronto, Canada
1 August 1994

I

A SKETCH OF HIS LIFE

Bertrand Arthur William Russell (after 1931 the 3rd Earl Russell) was born in Ravenscroft, the home of his parents near Trelleck in Wales, during the afternoon of 18 May 1872. His father was John Russell, Viscount Amberley, the eldest son of Lord John Russell (later 1st Earl Russell) of Reform Bill fame; his mother had been Kate Stanley before her marriage. Her father, the 2nd Baron Stanley of Alderley, was prominent, as were the Russells, in the Whig aristocracy. Lord and Lady Amberley held advanced opinions for their time, espousing such causes as free-thinking in religion, birth-control within marriage, and women's suffrage. Their stated intention was to educate their children in accord with their beliefs, but their elder son, Frank, proved unmanageable and had to be sent away to boarding school, and they were both dead before Bertrand's education commenced. Lady Amberley died from diphtheria, which she caught while nursing her daughter, who also died from the disease. His wife's death left Amberley with no will to live; unable or (what may be more likely) unwilling to shake off his melancholy, he grew gradually weaker; in this weakened state he fell victim to bronchitis, which killed him. On 9 January 1876, just eighteen months after his wife and daughter, he died at home, his sons having

1

been taken to his bedside for a final farewell. In his will he appointed two atheists as guardians of his sons, but the Russells successfully contested the will and had the boys declared wards of Chancery with custody granted to them. Thus it came to pass that Bertrand Russell was educated by a succession of governesses and tutors, as well as by his grandmother, his Aunt Agatha and his Uncle Rollo, in Pembroke Lodge, the Russells' grace -and-favour mansion in Richmond Park, on the edge of London.

Since the reign of Henry VIII members of the Russell family had been active in the service of the state, but with Amberley dead and the other adult males ineligible for one reason or other, and with Frank showing every sign of being an unpredictable adventurer, the family's hopes – or perhaps it was only his grandmother's hopes – settled upon Bertrand. He must be trained to carry on the family tradition, and then perhaps one day he too would become a reforming Prime Minister. She saw to it therefore that his education was broad: for, in addition to mathematics which he found delicious, he must know history, especially the role of the Whigs in it; English literature, in order to develop a good prose style; science, because it underlay the progress Lady Russell and her fellow Victorians took for granted; and French, German and Italian, in order one day to be able to conduct affairs of state with foreigners in their own languages.

His early life was one of great ease. Besides himself, there were living in Pembroke Lodge, after his grand-father's death in 1878, his grandmother, his aunt and his uncle. Frank was there only for school vacations. To look after the family there were eleven servants, so no Russell ever had to do any ordinary household chore. To tend to Bertrand and see to his intellectual development, there was a succession of governesses (in the earlier years) and tutors (in the later years), nearly all of them foreigners. None of them stayed very long, because Lady Russell did not want Bertrand unduly influenced by anyone but herself and her children. When there were signs that Bertrand and a tutor were developing a personal relationship, the tutor was dismissed, often without being allowed to bid Bertrand goodbye: at lesson time there would simply be a new tutor.

By his early teens it had become apparent to all that he was intelligent; the first recognition of it had come when he was eleven and his brother undertook to teach him Euclidean geometry. 'This was one of the great events of my life as dazzling as first love. I had not imagined that there was anything so delicious in the world. After I had learned the fifth proposition, my brother told me that it was generally considered difficult, but I had found no difficulty whatever. This was the first time it had dawned upon me that I might have some intelligence' (*1967, 36, 1967a, 37–8*). It was decided that he must go to university, but every university in those days required a knowledge of Greek and Latin for admission. Although he had a smattering of each, more was required. The drastic expedient hit upon was to send him to an Army crammer's school in London. Despite the fact that he was shocked by the gross behaviour of some of his classmates, the first people of his own generation with whom he had extensive association and nearly all of whom were destined for military careers, he flourished sufficiently to pass the entrance examination to Cambridge and even won a minor scholarship.

His early bent towards mathematics had proven to be his major talent and he enrolled at Cambridge in the autumn of 1890 in the Mathematical Tripos. He had been lucky in having Alfred North Whitehead read his scholarship examination. Whitehead saw more ability displayed in Russell's work than in that of any other candidate, although another man had earned a higher mark. Acting upon his judgment regarding talent and ability, Whitehead burnt all the papers and recommended Russell for the scholarship over the other man.

Whitehead rendered him another, more personal favour; he made a point of telling some of the abler students about Russell and encouraged them to seek him out. They did so, and Russell was delighted to discover that there were people to whom he could speak his mind without fear of ridicule, a reaction he had come to dread from his grandmother. His shyness and priggishness began to fade, and he found that he enjoyed, and was adept at, the give and take of intellectual debate. Some of those he met were members of the Apostles, a secret society dedicated to the free and open discussion of any topic on which a member chose to write a paper. After his election to the society Russell became a very active member and ever afterwards allowed that participation in its discussions was of cardinal importance in his education. All of the surviving papers he wrote for the society have now been published in *Cambridge Essays* (1983).

Russell differed from his fellow undergraduates in one important respect: they had no serious romantic attachments to women, but he did. In the summer of 1889, when he was only seventeen, he had met and fallen in love with Alys Whitall Smith, the younger daughter of Philadelphia Quakers turned religious revivalists, the Pearsall Smiths, who were then living in England. Five years his elder, she was a graduate of Bryn Mawr College and held advanced opinions, especially regarding the role of women in society. Although not quite love at first sight, the relationship did enmesh them both from the start, and during his years at Cambridge it developed and deepened. Despite strong Russell family opposition, which took the form of his grandmother opening the family closet to disclose a streak of madness hidden there, the couple were married on 13 December 1894. For the next several years they were, as they both later testified, very happy. For some months they lived in Berlin, studying German social democracy; they visited the United States, where Alys's family connections eased his entry into intellectual circles; and they led active social and political lives in England, always on the reforming side of any issue in which they took an interest.

Russell completed the work of the Mathematical Tripos in the spring of 1893. Although, as was later apparent, he was the ablest member of his class, he did not come out at the top, rather he was tied for seventh place. His failure to place higher may be due to the fact that he found the way mathematics was taught at Cambridge profoundly unsatisfactory. Nearly all the 'proofs' were, in his settled opinion, fallacious, because they appealed to principles which were assumed but not stated and defended. An elementary example is the use of superposition of figures in the proofs of some theorems in Euclidean geometry. Nowhere in the textbooks of the time was it laid down that a figure lifted through the third dimension retained its shape, yet this must be the case if a proof based upon the superposition of figures is to be valid. Russell was developing into a critic of mathematics, a characteristic not tested in examinations, so his marks were lower than those who had no doubts about what they had been taught and had learned it well. In later years he often repeated this criticism of the Tripos, and when he turned his attention to educational theory he made a critique of examinations an important part of it.

Foundational work in any branch of knowledge requires a knowledge of philosophy, and by the time he finished his mathematical degree Russell had come to realize this. Accordingly, he stayed on at Cambridge for a year of study in the Moral Sciences Tripos. During that year he studied the core of philosophy: its modern history, epistemology, metaphysics and ethics. The papers he wrote for his tutors have also been published in *Cambridge Essays*; they show him developing the critical skills without which his subsequent work would have been impossible. In the examinations for this Tripos he was awarded First Class Honours.

In the Cambridge of his day post-baccalaureate work was restricted to writing a dissertation which, if its examiners so recommended, led to election as a Fellow in the College to which it had been submitted. If no favourable recommendation was made, the candidate had no recognition for his work but had presumably benefited from the exercise and might be offered a teaching position elsewhere. Russell decided to try for a Fellowship at Trinity, his undergraduate college, but he was uncertain whether to write a thesis on the foundations of geometry, which one of his philosophy teachers urged him to do, or in economics, a subject in which he had no formal training but in which he was increasingly interested. After much thought, he decided upon the former topic largely because he could make use of what he had learned in both of his Triposes. He did not immediately abandon the study of economics, however, although he proved to be more interested in its political than its mathematical side. His first book, *German Social Democracy* (1896), is an early fruit of this study; it was published a year before *An Essay on the Foundations of Geometry* (1897), the book he made from his successful Fellowship dissertation.

Early in 1902 Russell suddenly realized that he was no longer in love with Alys, but to save appearances they agreed to share living quarters, an arrangement which continued for the next eight or nine years. Both led celibate lives, but, with the exception of a few friends and relatives, to the world at large they seemed a contented married couple. It was during these trying years that *Principia Mathematica* (1910–13) was written, and he poured into that great work all of his pent-up passion. After his work on that book was done, Russell accepted an appointment as lecturer at Cambridge for five years beginning in October 1910. Rooms in Trinity College were included, a welcome perquisite for a man whose marriage lay in ruins.

In 1910, while canvassing votes for her husband Philip, a Liberal member of Parliament, Russell got to know Lady Ottoline Morrell, the half-sister of the 6th Duke of Portland. A shared aristocratic upbringing was to make for an easier relationship than the one he had had with Alys. A year later, while Russell was staying in her London house on his way to Paris, their friendship was suddenly transformed into a love affair, and for the next five years she was the centre of his life. Since she refused to leave her husband, their affair was, to a large extent, carried on in letters, with the occasional clandestine meeting. Over 3500 letters were exchanged between them. On his side Russell poured out his heart and mind to her; his letters document how hard he tried to please her. While under her influence he even attempted writing fiction and quasi-religious prose, both of which were abandoned when it became obvious that he had almost no talent for them. The bits that survive have been published in *Contemplation and Action* (1985).

When the First World War broke out Lady Ottoline stood by him in his opposition to it. During the war, their affair gradually cooled into friendship, and he turned to casual philandering; the flow of letters continued, although now she was not told everything. Anti-war work absorbed a great deal of his energy; he spent part of most days at the offices of the No-Conscription Fellowship performing all sorts of thankless tasks. A leaflet he wrote for this organization in 1916 led to his being charged in court with interfering with the recruitment of soldiers. He was tried, convicted and fined £100; the fine was collected by the forced sale of some of his possessions. But he lost very little by the judgment, since his friends bought all of his most valuable articles, including some 1500 books, and returned them to him.

Shortly after his trial Russell went to the Lavender Hill police station in south London to offer Clifford Allen, the chairman of the No-Conscription Fellowship, moral support when he turned himself in to face a charge of desertion. There Russell met Lady Constance Malleson, an actress whose stage name was Colette O'Niel, who had come for the same reason. She was not quite twenty-one; Russell was forty-four. She was a daughter of the 5th Earl Annesley, so again a shared background made relations easy. Two months later their paths crossed again, not altogether by chance as Colette later confessed, and they became lovers. At the time she was married to Miles Malleson, the playwright and actor, but they had agreed, before they entered into it, that marriage should not preclude affairs. Russell tried without success to persuade her that they both seek divorces and marry. He wanted children and, as heir to an earldom, he wanted them to be legitimate. Colette did not want children, and, as he became convinced that she was sincere, his ardour cooled. For about four years, however, she was the woman in his life, and even after he abandoned her for another there were occasional reconciliations. For her part she remained in love with him for the rest of her life.

During the summer of 1919 Russell met (for the second time) and began an affair with Dora Black, a young and vigorous Fellow of Girton College, Cambridge, who wanted children as much as he did. For some months their relationship endured separations; she was studying in Paris and then he was off on a visit to the infant Soviet Union where she followed him on her own. When he accepted an invitation to teach for a year in China he asked her to accompany him. Despite the fact that he was still married to Alys, they lived openly together, and before the year was out Dora was pregnant. Alys was appealed to for a divorce; she obliged, and it became final on 21 September 1921. The marriage took place six days later, and John Conrad, whom Russell named in memory of his father and the novelist, Joseph Conrad, was born on 16 November. Katharine, named for his mother, was born two years later.

With a family to provide for and children to educate, he turned his hand to writing for the popular press, churning out articles to order and never missing a deadline. Wartime journalism proved excellent practice for the writing he was now obliged to do to earn his living. In addition to articles for newspapers and magazines, he wrote popular books on a wide variety of topics, all of which earned him money. To educate their children the Russells decided to open their own school, since no existing school seemed to them quite good enough. Beacon Hill School greatly increased the need for money and, finding that their writings alone (Dora had taken up journalism too) did not provide enough, both of them undertook exhausting lecture tours of the United States to raise funds.

The pressures generated in running and funding a school, and the strains produced by their extra-marital affairs, about which they were in theoretical agreement, gradually led to the disintegration of their marriage and forced a separation. The breaking point came after Dora gave birth to two children fathered by an American journalist. Dora remained with the school and kept it going into the Second World War when it was closed. Before their separation Russell had taken up with Patricia (Peter) Spence, an Oxford under-graduate whom Dora had hired as a governess for John and Kate. The process of obtaining a divorce and reaching an agreement on custody of the children was a long and disagreeable one. The divorce became final in 1935, and he and Peter were married in January 1936. A son, Conrad, also named for the novelist, was born in 1937; Conrad, a distinguished British historian, is now the 5th Earl Russell, having succeeded his half-brother, who had no sons, in 1987.

After his divorce and remarriage, Russell's financial situation was even more strained: he had £300 unearned income and had to pay £800 to other people, so he had to find a way to earn more than his writing alone would bring him. The solution he hit upon was to return to philosophical work and take a teaching position. The first offer he received, which he gladly accepted, was from the University of Chicago for the academic year 1938–9. During the course of his year in Chicago, he was offered and accepted a three-year appointment in the University of California at Los Angeles; and, during his first year there, he received an offer of appointment from the College of the City of New York to commence in the fall of 1940. The prospect of living in New York City greatly appealed to him, so he resigned from UCLA and accepted CCNY's offer. This proved to be a disastrous mistake. Much of the Christian clergy in New York rose up against him; the educational authorities defended his appointment, but in the end Mayor Laguardia undercut them by a line veto of Russell's salary in the city budget. The whole unsavoury story is well told by Paul Edwards in an appendix to *Why I Am Not a Christian* (1957).

Stranded in the United States with only his American royalties as income and unable to return to England because of wartime travel restrictions, he turned to his fellow philosophers for help. Through the good offices of John Dewey an eccentric millionaire came to his rescue. Albert C. Barnes, who made his fortune from Argyrol, had amassed a stunning collection of paintings, most of them by Impressionist and Post-Impressionist painters, published books on the art of painting, and founded a school to disseminate his ideas about art. Although Russell knew Barnes to be something of a crank, he was nevertheless glad to accept when Barnes offered him a five-year contract worth $40,000 to deliver one lecture a week on the history of Western philosophy, starting at its inception and ending with Russell's own philosophy. The relationship proved a stormy one and was abruptly terminated by Barnes in November 1942, with three years to run. As his grounds for dismissing Russell Barnes charged that Russell, by accepting outside speaking engagements, had breached his contract with the Barnes Foundation. Russell in turn sued Barnes for breach of contract and won; Barnes was ordered to pay him $20,000 of the $24,000 outstanding on his contract. In addition to this windfall, the Barnes episode generated another. The book of his lectures, *A History of Western Philosophy*, was his first bestseller; its publication in 1945 put an end to his financial worries once and for all.

It was not until May 1944 that Russell was able to book passage home. His return to England was brightened by a five-year lectureship at Trinity College; he was also made a Fellow (later a life Fellow) and given rooms with which he was delighted. During these years in Cambridge he wrote his last major philosophical book, *Human Knowledge: Its Scope and Limits* (1948), and became a major attraction on the BBC. Two outstanding awards also came to him: the Order of Merit (which is limited to twenty-four living members) in 1949 and the Nobel Prize for Literature in 1950. But in his personal life he was less fortunate; his marriage to Peter came to an end in 1949 with the bitterness such breaks usually entailed for him. After their divorce was final he married for the last time in 1952. Edith Finch was an American with strong ties to Bryn Mawr College. Through friends she had made there she had come to know Alys Russell, but this tie with his ancient past did not, as it well might have done, present an obstacle. In his *Autobiography* (1967–9), which is dedicated to Edith, he stated that their marriage was all he could have hoped it to be.

The last two decades of his life were devoted to autobiography and political activism. For the BBC he broadcast superb epitomes of his life and the lives of others he had known, and for the record he wrote *My Philosophical Development* (1959); he also published his *Autobiography*, the first two volumes of which he had written in the early 1930s and which he had put into final form during his last residence in Cambridge; the third was assembled, with considerable help from Edith and others, in the late 1960s. From Christmas 1954, when he broadcast 'Man's Peril from the H-Bomb', to his death, the greater part of his time was given over to agitation against nuclear war. During these years he acquired a full-time secretary for the first time in his life, a circumstance which greatly facilitated the flow of messages from his home. The last one was signed on 31 January 1970; he died between 7:00 and 8:00 p.m. on 2 February, protesting to the end.

II
LOGIC AND THE FOUNDATIONS OF MATHEMATICS

His Fellowship dissertation on the foundations of geometry did not, in his later opinion, make any lasting contribution to its subject. Undertaken at the urging of James Ward, one of his teachers in the Moral Sciences Tripos, it was heavily influenced by the Kantian philosophy and arrived at conclusions that were soon shown to be false. 'The geometry in Einstein's General Theory of Relativity is such as I had declared to be impossible.' Except in some of its details he did not think 'there is anything valid in this early work' (*1959*, 40).

After turning his thesis into a book, he decided to make a companion study of the foundations of physics, but it was soon apparent to him that foundational work in physics presupposed that similar work had previously been completed in mathematics. A survey of the literature showed that such work had not been done, so he decided to undertake it himself. Over the next few years, he worked diligently, producing draft after draft of a book on the foundations of mathematics. He learnt by his failures, and when in 1900 he attended a philosophical congress in Paris he recognized at once that Giuseppe Peano, an Italian mathematician, with much to say in the discussions, had the clearest conception of the questions at issue and the best vocabulary for talking about them. Russell asked Peano for copies of his writings, which he studied with great care; he found they provided him with solutions to a number of the problems he had encountered in his own work.

Before he discovered Peano's works he had convinced himself that the foundations of mathematics were to be found in logic. Logic was enjoying a renaissance in the late nineteenth century; it had been transformed through the work of George Boole, Augustus De Morgan, Charles Sanders Peirce and others into a purely symbolic science. Many complicated arguments, long intuitively felt to be valid, were revealing their structure and their validity under the new techniques. For instance, the obviously valid argument, 'Horses are animals, therefore, the head of a horse is the head of an animal', which had resisted all attempts to recast it as a syllogism, is easily proved valid in the new logic. The long supremacy of the syllogism was over; in the new logic the logic of the syllogism occupied a significant, but fairly early, place in the whole subject. Russell was aware of some of these developments; he was therefore in a position to appreciate the systemization Peano and his school were bringing to the subject.

From his reading of Peano's works he learnt of many new advances in symbolic logic and also of Peano's set of axioms for arithmetic, which leaves only three terms undefined. These axioms are: '(1) 0 is a number; (2) The successor of any number is a number; (3) No two numbers have the same successor; (4) 0 is not the successor of any number; (5) Any property which belongs to 0, and also to the successor of any number which has the property, belongs to all numbers' (*1919*,

5–6). All of the words in these axioms, with the exception of '0', 'number' and 'successor', are logical words which (with a single exception) had been studied by the symbolic logicians. (The single exception was 'the' in the singular, to which we shall return later.) Therefore, if Peano's three undefined terms could be given purely logical definitions and 'the' successfully analyzed, and the restated axioms proved using only logical truths as premises, then the arithmetic of the natural numbers would have been shown to be a branch of logic. Russell set himself the task of finding definitions of the required kind for these three terms; he succeeded in analyzing 'the' and in constructing definitions for '0' and 'number'; the definition of 'successor' he found had been given by Gottlob Frege some years earlier in a work which Russell studied only after his own work was far advanced. Since Frege had also defined '0' and 'number' in a way equivalent to Russell's definitions, the definition which will now be outlined is usually referred to as the Frege-Russell definition of 'number'.

The natural numbers, which are also called the finite cardinals, are the numbers we use in counting; they are used to answer the question, 'How many?' Since they carry neither positive nor negative signs, the only operations which can be performed on them are addition and multiplication. The other operations commonly thought to be arithmetical, subtraction and division, require numbers of different kinds: subtraction demands signed numbers, or the positive and negative integers; and division requires rational real numbers, or fractions. Definitions of these other kinds of numbers are based on the definition of 'natural number'. This definition, therefore, is important for the whole theory of numbers. Since '0' is a number, a definition of 'number' leads to a definition of '0', leaving only 'successor' to be defined to complete the translation of Peano's axioms into logical notation.

In thinking about the way we use these numbers Russell noticed that they are always applied to classes; the number 2, for example, is always a predicate of a pair, a pair being a class with two members. Uses of the number 2 seem to have only this property in common. This observation is the basis of his definition of 'number' and of '0', '1', '2', etc. The basic idea is that of a one-to-one correspondence. When we count any collection of objects we put the numbers into a one-to-one correspondence with the objects in the set; when we have put one number against each member we have the number of things in the collection. There are relations other than that used in counting which are one-to-one; the marriage relation in monogamous countries provides an example; in such countries we know without counting that there are the same number of wives as husbands. Even though 'one' occurs in our designation for the one-to-one relation, it can be defined without using 'one'. 'A relation is said to be "one-one" when, if x has the relation in question to y, no other term x' has the same relation to y, and x does not have the same relation to any term y' other than y' (*1919*, 15). This definition looks complicated but everyone who has learned to count understands it. Once we have used a number to count a member of a class, we cannot use that number again to count another member of the same class, nor can we apply a fresh number to a member we have already counted. Only very small children make these mistakes.

The next step in the process of definition is to introduce the notion of a similar class. A class *A* is said to be 'similar' to a class *B* if there exists a one-to-one relationship between the members of *A* and the members of *B*. Thus the class of husbands is similar to the class of wives in monogamous countries. With this definition in mind it is easy to see that any classes which are similar will have the same number of members. Using this common characteristic, we can then form classes of similar classes; one such is the class of all couples; another the class of all triplets. We are now in a position to define 'the number of a class': 'The number of a class is the class of all those classes that are similar to it' (*1919*, 18). From this definition it follows immediately that 2 is the class of all couples, because 2 is the number of a couple. A couple, it should be noted, can be defined without using 'two'; a couple consists of any *x* and any *y* which are not identical to each other. Definitions of the other numbers follow equally directly: 0 is the class whose sole member is the empty (or null) class; 1 is the class of all unit classes; 3 is the class of all triplets; and so on. And 'number' itself can be defined: 'A number is anything which is the number of some class' (*1919*, 19). Although this definition has the appearance of circularity, it is not circular. This can be seen by examining the definition of 'the number of a class'; it is defined without any mention of 'number'. Russell went on to show that 'number' and the various numbers, so defined, have all the properties mathematicians expect such entities to have; thus the definitions are justified.

The steps which he went through in reaching a definition of 'number' are typical of the way definitions are introduced in symbolic logic. Russell first defined a 'one-one relation' in purely logical terms; then 'similar classes' in terms of 'one-one relations'; then 'the number of a class' in terms of 'similar classes'; and finally 'number' in terms of 'the number of a class'. In *Principia Mathematica*, where these definitions are laid out using only symbols, it is possible, by working back through the chain of definitions, to write the definition of 'number' in language of the level used to define 'one-one relation'; but it would be undertaken by a logician only if he suspected a fallacy had crept in at some stage. The point of introducing definitions at crucial steps in the development of a system is to keep the enterprise manageable. (The hierarchy of definitions is something like the hierarchy of political divisions that have evolved; in North America, for example, they reach from house-holds through school districts, townships and towns, counties, states and provinces, to the federal government itself. Such groupings also facilitate management.) The definitions should, of course, be studied at their first introduction until they are understood, but, once understood, they are simply used to reach the next stage where they will in turn disappear as part of the definition of something more complicated.

The notion of a class is clearly central to the definition of 'number'. In the course of his work on *The Principles of Mathematics* (1903), where the definition is first reported, he made a very unwelcome discovery concerning classes. Georg Cantor, in a work Russell was studying, gave a proof that there is no greatest cardinal number. Russell thought the proof must be fallacious, because it contradicted what seemed obvious to him, namely, that the number of things in the universe must be the greatest cardinal number.

Therefore, he decided to apply Cantor's proof to this number in order to expose the fallacy he believed it committed. Application of the proof necessarily involved the concept of class, for it was known that, given any number of things, the number of classes they give rise to is greater than their number. Given three things, eight classes are realized: the empty or null class, three classes with one different member each, three classes with two members each, and, finally, a class containing all three as members. In general n things form 2^n classes. Russell had, then, to consider classes, if he wanted to think about the largest number to which the things in the world gives rise. This exercise led him to the discovery of a very interesting class.

In daily life when we consider a class, we form it, almost without thinking of what we are doing, by putting into it everything having a certain predicate. Thus the class of rare books has in it all and only those things of which it is true to say that it is a rare book. The principle used here, called by logicians 'the principle of extensionality', seems utterly obvious. Everyone who had written about classes, up to and including Frege, had assumed it without argument. 'Every predicate determines a class' was treated as an article of common sense. Now one of the predicates we use is 'class' itself, and it was a consideration of it that Russell believed would provide a refutation of Cantor. Applying the principle of extensionality to 'x is a class' leads directly to the class of all classes. He noticed that this great class contained two different sorts of classes: classes that are not members of themselves, of which the class of rare books is an instance, since the class of rare books is not itself a rare book; and classes that are members of themselves, of which the class of non-books is an example, for the class of non-books is itself a non-book and so is a member of itself. His attention settled upon the first kind, which he called 'ordinary classes'. Since all of them have a predicate in common, namely, 'x is not a member of x' or 'x is an ordinary class', they form a class, the class of all classes that are not members of themselves, which we will call O, to remind ourselves that it is the class of all ordinary classes. Having formed this class Russell asked himself: 'Is O a member of O or not?' and came to an astonishing conclusion. On the one hand, if we assume that O is a member of O, then it follows that O is an ordinary class; but no ordinary class is a member of itself, therefore O is not a member of O. On the other hand, if we assume that O is not a member of O, then it follows that O is an ordinary class, because it is not a member of itself; therefore O is a member of O. Putting the two parts of the argument together, we reach the conclusion that O is a member of O, if and only if, O is not a member of O. This is as flat a contradiction as is possible, yet it follows from the common-sensical notion of 'class'. Since its publication in 1903 this contradiction has been known as 'Russell's paradox'.

Discovery of the paradox brought his work to an abrupt halt, because one of the fundamental principles involved, the principle of extensionality, had been shown to have a fatal flaw. It led directly to a contradiction, and since from a contradiction any proposition whatever can be 'proved' deductively, it follows that, if the extensionality principle is retained unmodified, all mathematical propositions, both the true and the false, can be 'proved' as theorems of the system. This will not do. Some change is demanded, but it is not at all apparent what change will tame the principle without also eliminating some of its benign uses. Communication of the paradox to his fellow workers caused grave concern. Frege replied that his life's work lay in ruins and that arithmetic itself was tottering. Whitehead failed to cheer Russell by telegraphing a line from Browning's 'The Lost Leader': 'Never glad, confident morning again.'

Russell's solution to the paradox, which he sketched in an appendix to *The Principles of Mathematics* and later developed into a full-fledged theory, is called 'the theory of types'. The germinal idea for this theory is that the root of the difficulty stems from an unrestricted use of the self-membership relation. If self-membership were prohibited, then the paradox would not arise. If this plan were adopted, then no class could be a member of itself, which goes somewhat counter to our intuition that the class of abstract ideas, say, is itself an abstract idea. After examining many alternatives with what he thought had more serious defects, he developed a theory which proscribed self-membership. A hierarchy of types was proposed, the lowest type being that of individuals, the next consisting of classes of individuals, the next encompassing classes of classes of individuals, and so on, with the membership relation holding only between members of a lower and next higher type. The membership relation is prohibited between members of the same type. This is only the barest sketch of his theory, but even this outline allows one to glimpse the enormous complication to logic which he thought was necessary to tame his paradox. The complication introduced by the theory of types has led others to propose solutions which do not require such an elaborate edifice.

The Principles of Mathematics   argues the philosophical case for logicism, the thesis, baldly stated, that
mathematics (or at least an important part of it) is a
branch of logic. In his preface he promised a second
volume in which a constructive proof of the thesis
would be presented, all symbolically developed, and he
announced with great pleasure that Alfred North
Whitehead had agreed to be co-author of the projected
second volume. In 1898 Whitehead had published the
first volume of *A Treatise on Universal Algebra*, the
second volume of which promised to develop the thesis
of the first in a more systematic and symbolic way.
While reading Russell's book before publication,
Whitehead realized they were engaged in similar
projects and suggested they join forces; thus began one
of the most important collaborations in the history of
science.

The Principles of Mathematics was published in 1903
and the first volume of their joint work, *Principia
Mathematica*, came out in 1910. The project had
outgrown its early conception as a second volume of
Principles. Its authors had to bring together in one
symbolic language the work of many earlier students in
logic and the foundations of mathematics; they had to
discover a set of axioms for logic itself; they had to
prove that their axioms validated known logical truths;
they had to devise ways of reporting these proofs; they
had to keep the language manageable by introducing
abbreviating definitions, of the sort discussed above, at
appropriate places in the chain of proofs; and they had
to write it all down. In about equal parts *Principia* is a
work of analysis and a work of synthesis. Many
analytical problems had to be solved in the course of its
generation – one of them, the problem of the proper

analysis of definite descriptions – will be given in the next chapter; and much synthesis of the original work of others had to be effected in order to fit the fruits of their work into the grand architectonic being erected. The publication of the first volume established, at a stroke, the discipline commonly called symbolic or mathematical logic. Two more volumes were published later, but in the end the work remained incomplete. Whitehead was to write a fourth volume incorporating geometry into the system, but, although at one time most of it existed in manuscript, it was never published, and all his manuscripts were burnt by his wife, acting on his instructions, after his death.

Principia Mathematica offers a very detailed proof of the logicist thesis that an important part of mathematics is a branch of logic. By making their assumptions explicit, Whitehead and Russell offered the critics of logicism a clear focus for their attacks. Two rival schools, the formalists and the intuitionists, were working on questions in the foundations of mathematics at this time Members of both groups disputed the claims of Whitehead and Russell. The controversy over the foundations of mathematics generated a large literature, which continues to grow today. In 1925, when a second edition of *Principia* was called for, Whitehead requested that Russell alone write the new introduction. In the first paragraph of his introduction Russell announced his decision not to alter the body of the work, but instead to offer 'the main improvements which appear desirable'; he goes on to note that 'some of these are scarcely open to question; others are, as yet, a matter of opinion'. This proved to be his last contribution to the controversy over the foundations of mathematics. In later years logicism had defenders who offered more elegant systems than that to be found in *Principia*, but these systems would not have been possible had that book not gone before.

III
SCIENTIFIC METHOD IN PHILOSOPHY

In philosophy Russell nearly always claimed that he had more confidence in the correctness of his method than he did in the truth of the conclusions he reached applying that method. After early attempts, soon abandoned, to use the Hegelian method on problems in the philosophy of physics and the philosophy of mathematics, he settled upon analysis as his philosophical method. In his book on Leibniz, published in 1900, he opened a chapter with the pronouncement 'That all sound philosophy should begin with an analysis of propositions, is a truth too evident, perhaps, to demand a proof' (1900, 8). Despite his claim of self-evidence, most philosophers of the time would not have agreed with this assertion, but G. E. Moore (and a few others) did share his view. By the impressive quality of the results they obtained through use of the method of analysis, Moore and Russell gradually convinced the younger generation of philosophers of the power of analysis and its superiority to any other known method.

In 1900 the tools available for the analysis of propositions were not many. The chapter from which the quoted sentence is taken made use of no tool in its analysis of the law of contradiction and other necessary propositions which was not available to Leibniz two hundred years earlier. The paucity of analytical tools was a problem of which Russell soon became very conscious. While he was working through the various drafts of *The Principles of Mathematics* he searched for advances in logical technique which would facilitate the analysis of mathematical propositions. He was rewarded beyond his expectations when he heard Peano speak at a philosophical congress in Paris in 1900. Peano and his followers had developed very powerful symbolic techniques for the analysis of arithmetical statements. Russell studied their publications and adopted their tools; he did not discover the work of Frege (some of which he duplicated) until his own book was finished. In a long appendix he called attention to Frege's work and wrote that it was 'philosophically very superior' (*1903*, *501*) to Peano's, but that its notation was inferior to Peano's and that it proved cumbersome in use.

The new analytical tools he fell heir to, or developed on his own, during his early work on the foundations of mathematics, and the use of them in *The Principles of Mathematics*, make that book a transitional one in his development. A few years after it was published he came to think of it as not very precise. The interval had seen explosive growth in logic, and some of the important advances had been contributed by Russell himself. Many concepts which had remained unanalyzed throughout their use in mathematics were given analytical definitions in *Principia Mathematica* and assigned a precise place in its structure. They were available for any philosopher to use, but there was a hitch: to use them a philosopher had to be highly trained in mathematical logic and not many were, even decades after the publication of *Principia*. Russell, and a very few of his pupils, had the use of the new techniques pretty much to themselves in the early years.

During the course of his work with Whitehead on *Principia*, Russell continued to focus on propositional analysis as the key to removing the obstacles he found in his way. His theory of definite descriptions, to be sketched later, arose from his attempts to provide an analysis of propositions of the sort 'the present Pope is a Pole'. In reflecting upon the procedures he had in fact followed in his successful analyses, he gradually came to realize that the method of analysis, as he practiced it, did not differ significantly from scientific method. Recognition of a problem is the first step: it consists in noticing that certain facts, or puzzling propositions, require explanation. The next is to search for other facts of a similar kind. In collecting facts one should try to find the most striking ones available, for such a collection is more stimulating both to the imagination and to the intellect. 'A logical theory may be tested by its capacity for dealing with puzzles, and it is a wholesome plan, in thinking about logic, to stock the mind with as many puzzles as possible, since these serve much the same purpose as is served by experiments in physical science' (*1956*, 47). Making such collections is bound to be a haphazard undertaking, for as yet the researcher has no hypothesis, or at best a rudimentary one, to guide the search. Russell's collection of paradoxes, with which he began his 1908 paper on the theory of types, serves as a fine example of this initial step (*1956*, 59–61); the sources he cites for the paradoxes show that some came to him by chance and others by a search of the literature. Once a collection of unexplained facts is to hand, the next step is to try to come up with an hypothesis explanatory of some or all of them. During this period any and every analytical tool that promises help is brought to bear on the individual facts in an attempt to uncover their common features. If common characteristics are found, an important step toward a solution has been taken, for it may prove possible to formulate an hypothesis which will account for the common features. If a hypothesis is found, it then becomes the centre of attention, because hypotheses seldom occur to researchers in their final form; they have usually to be adjusted, tested and refined.

Reflecting on the steps he found himself taking while using his method, Russell noticed a striking similarity between his method and that used by scientists. To emphasize the common features he called his method 'the scientific method in philosophy'. Most philosophers of the time believed that a special method, derived in large part from the Hegelian tradition, was required in philosophy; he thought they were mistaken in this belief. All genuine philosophical problems could be solved by application of the scientific method; those problems not amenable to it, he was inclined to think, were not genuine problems at all. Here is an early instance of the belief, so attractive to the logical positivists and others, that some so-called philosophical problems are pseudo-problems.

The first fruits of his reflections regarding method were, as was his wont during this period of his life, outlined in a letter to Lady Ottoline of 8 March 1912. With George Geach, one of his pupils, he had gone for a walk.

> I began to talk about how philosophy should be studied – how people ought to have more of the scientific impulse for collecting queer facts, less fear of spending their time on

characteristics which mark all of its propositions. In the first place a philosophical proposition is *general*: 'It must not deal specially with things on the surface of the earth, or with the solar system, or with any other portion of space and time.' In the second place, philosophical propositions are *a priori*; they 'must be such as can be neither proved nor disproved by empirical evidence'. Taken together they yield a definition of 'philosophy': 'philosophy is the science of the possible.' Another way to make the same point is to say that philosophy is 'indistinguishable from logic as that word has now come to be used', because logic, as practiced by Russell, is concerned (1) with discovering general propositions which talk about everything without mentioning anything in particular, and (2) with analyzing and enumerating logical forms. An example of (1) is 'if x is an M and x is identical with y, then y is an M, whatever x, y, and M may be'; (2) yields, for example, a catalogue of the kinds of propositions there are. 'The essence of philosophy as thus conceived is analysis, not synthesis. ... What is feasible is the understanding of general forms, and the division of traditional problems into a number of separate and less baffling questions. "Divide and conquer" is the maxim of success here as elsewhere' (*1918*, 113).

The use of scientific method in philosophy, as in science, requires a flow of fresh hypotheses to be tested. He was aware of this requirement of his method and had some advice to give, but, in the end, he like everyone else, had to admit that the process of generating new hypotheses is one about which little is known. His way, which proved successful on many occasions, was to begin by immersing himself in the problem to hand, reading what others had written about it and discussing it with anyone he met who was capable of understanding it. This period of intense concentration had, he thought, two desirable consequences: (1) it impresses the problem on the mind to the point where sub-conscious thought about it is likely to occur; (2) it eliminates a number of hypotheses that others have tried and found wanting. Once the period of concentrated attention on the problem was completed, he found it useful to do something entirely different – reading novels was one of his favourite diversions – in order to clear the problem from consciousness. Further conscious thought about it, he discovered, interfered with sub-conscious thought processes. If the process is successful, a time will come when the solution to the problem will come flooding into consciousness; then all that remains is to write it down.

There is no set of rules by use of which new hypotheses can be discovered: they occur to a mind prepared to receive them. He found that in his own work he had to discipline himself rather severely in the early stages of working on a problem. The discipline required was similar to that which mystics impose upon themselves, and in them he recognized kindred spirits. In 'Mysticism and Logic' he allowed that mystical insight is a fruitful source of hypotheses that may, when tested, prove to be true, but he criticized most mystics for failure to see the necessity of an independent test of truth. A fresh look at an old problem will sometimes yield an hypothesis, which its originator at the time feels must be true, but, Russell insisted, it still must be tested by the usual methods – thus the 'logic' in the title of the essay – before its truth can be taken as established.

The other question that bothered his critics was this: how do you know when to stop? Can not analysis go on, perhaps forever, with nothing to show for all the work? He had an answer for them. 'It may be laid down generally that *possibility* always marks insufficient analysis; when analysis is completed, only the *actual* can be relevant, for the simple reason that there is only the actual, and that the merely possible is nothing' (*1984*, 27). Analysis continues until the variables employed in the symbolic transformations of the original proposition denote actual entities. This ideal of analysis led him, on several occasions, to remark that an analysis of physical phenomena in terms of the sense-data of one person would please him most.

His demand that only actual entities be used in completed analyses is an example of his use of Occam's Razor. William of Occam, an English scholastic philosopher, laid it down that entities are not to be multiplied unnecessarily. Russell adopted this principle as central to his conception of analysis. Possible entities, if one were obliged to admit them, would clutter the universe. A philosopher can easily lose control of his explanations if entities are allowed to multiply without restriction. Russell was firm in his desire to control the number of *kinds* of entities he admitted. If an analysis of a statement mentioning a class can be given which mentions only the members of the class, then, in his view, a real advance has been made. The analysis shows that classes can be constructed out of their members and that there is no need to regard them as entities having ontological status. As he put it, they are 'logical constructions' or 'logical fictions'. We can still go on using them, but we are no longer obliged to believe they have independent being. 'Wherever possible, logical constructions are to be substituted for inferred entities' he called 'the supreme maxim in scientific philosophising' (*1918*, 155). An inferred entity is one whose existence is postulated in order to explain certain observable effects (which are then attributed to its activity). Trails in cloud chambers lead to the postulated existence of particles whose movement produces the trails; the existence of other people's minds is arrived at by similar reasoning. His method would have us attempt to construct the physical particle out of its effects; when successfully completed we are in a position to say that the particle is its effects (suitably organized, of course, by mathematical logic). Similarly, what we might mean by another's mind is the behaviour we observe, again with its logical complications preserved. If such analyses can be carried out, an ontological gain has been made. We are no longer obliged to postulate the existence of entities of which we have no experience, but – and this is his point in calling such entities 'logical fictions' – we can still use such words and phrases as 'electron' and 'your mind' in talking and writing about our experience, only now we understand such expressions to be mere shorthand for very complicated logical constructions. Logical fictions are entities which have been stripped of their metaphysical baggage.

Russell believed his method to be a potent weapon against metaphysical excesses. Although many of the problems he tried to solve are usually classified as metaphysical, he never seemed to regard himself as a metaphysician. He thought of himself, rather as a logician who was attempting to rescue some long-standing problems from the grips of the metaphysicians. He seemed to think that metaphysics, as traditionally conceived, was hardly respectable. This opinion grew in him during the years he devoted to the study of the foundations of mathematics. When he turned to the writings of philosophers for help on the problems he faced he found them worse than useless. 'Only those who have waded through the quagmire of philosophic speculation on this subject', he wrote of Zeno's paradoxes, 'can realize what a liberation from antique prejudices is involved in this simple and straightforward commonplace.' The commonplace is that 'motion consists merely in the fact that bodies are sometimes in one place and sometimes in another, and that they are at intermediate places at intermediate times' (*1918*, 84). Kant was one of the worst offenders; his philosophy of mathematics had to be discarded completely. 'The whole doctrine of *a priori* intuitions, by which Kant explained the possibility of pure mathematics, is wholly inapplicable to mathematics in its present form.' The present form of mathematics is expressed by saying that it is 'nothing but formal logic' (*1918*, 96). He found Kant wanting, not just in the philosophy of mathematics, but in most branches of philosophy. 'Kant has the reputation of being the greatest of modern philosophers, but to my mind he was a mere misfortune' (*1927a*, 83).

The philosophy of mathematics was not the only part of philosophy that had been ill-served by traditional metaphysics. Russell was, verbally at least, anti-metaphysical right across the board. In his critique of Karl Marx he argued that Marx's materialism is not required in most of the arguments in which Marx uses it. It is just as well for Marx that it is irrelevant: 'Whenever metaphysics is really useful in reaching a conclusion, that is because the conclusion cannot be reached by scientific means, i.e. because there is no good reason to suppose it true. What can be known, can be known without metaphysics, and whatever needs metaphysics for its proof cannot be proved' (*1934*, 227). Any philosopher who took metaphysics seriously earned Russell's scorn. 'The belief that metaphysics has any bearing upon practical affairs is, to my mind, a proof of logical incapacity' (*1934*, 226). The anti-metaphysical bias so prominent in the early logical positivists owed a great deal to Russell's propaganda against the subject.

IV
THE THEORY OF DESCRIPTIONS:
AN EXAMPLE OF HIS METHOD
IN USE

As an example of his use of scientific method in philosophy we will take his theory of definite descriptions. Although he published his theory several years before he wrote up his philosophical method, it is clear from the way he expounds his method that he was using it in his analysis of descriptions. A definite description is a phrase like 'the author of *The Principles of Mathematics*'. Such phrases are perplexing for the logician because they function like names in sentences. The police must resort to such phrases in their work, for until the perpetrator of a crime is identified the usual way of referring to him or her is by phrases like 'the murderer of Martin Luther King'. Indeed, everybody uses definite descriptions, for we more often than not do not know the names of those we talk about, but that does not stop us from gossiping about them. When definite descriptions uniquely refer no logical problems arise. But they do not always uniquely refer: Agatha Christie's *Murder on the Orient Express* provides a fine example of the use of the expression 'the murderer' to mislead the reader, for, as it turns out, there are many involved in the murder. Sometimes definite descriptions do not refer at all, as, for example, in talk of 'the pot of gold at the end of the rainbow'. In daily life we manage by correcting ourselves as we learn more about the world, but in mathematics Russell could not tolerate such uncertainty; he had to find a way to bring such referring expressions under logical control.

The traditional logic of the syllogism treated such expressions, when it noticed them at all, in the same way it handled proper names. 'All men are mortal; Socrates is a man; therefore, Socrates is mortal' is an instance of a valid syllogism. Now suppose 'Socrates' is replaced by 'the present king of Belgium'; clearly the syllogism remains valid. But what if we substitute 'the present king of France' for 'Socrates'? Since France is not a monarchy, the substitution creates a puzzle. 'The present king of France' purports to refer to one and only one person, but we know the reference fails. What then, if anything, does it refer to? Traditional logic, Russell found, had no answer to offer.

Phrases of the form 'the so-and-so' are commonly used in mathematics, for instances take 'the fourth root of equation A' or 'the class of all classes which are not members of themselves', and it was there that Russell first encountered them as a problem for analysis. To bring propositions of the form 'The so-and-so is such-and-such' into the symbolic language Whitehead and he were developing in their work on the foundations of mathematics required that such propositions be analyzed into the symbols already adopted, or, failing that, a new symbol for 'the so-and-so' would have to be introduced. The second alternative would be a last resort, because it would be an admission that a new kind of entity was required.

Russell began by collecting striking instances of the use of definite descriptions. Here are four of them (with a fifth for comparison):

(1) The golden mountain does not exist.
(2) The present king of France is bald.
(3) The present king of France is not bald.
(4) The author of *Waverley* is Scott.
(5) Scott is Scott.

The puzzling feature of (1) is that it seems both to be true and about the golden mountain, but if it is true then there is no golden mountain for it to be about, and if it is about the golden mountain then it is not true. (2) and (3) are puzzling when taken as a pair. According to the law of non-contradiction one of them must be true and the other false. 'Yet if we enumerated the things that are bald, and then the things that are not bald, we should not find the present king of France in either list. Hegelians, who love a synthesis, will probably conclude he wears a wig' (*1956*, 48). The feature of (4) which is perplexing is that it is both true and informative. It would, of course, be true, if 'the author of *Waverley*' meant 'Scott', as can be seen by (5), but then it would not be informative. But (4) is informative, since, as Russell notes, George IV asked whether Scott was the author of *Waverley*, which was a sensible question given the anonymous publication of the early novels in the series, but only an imbecile would ask whether Scott was Scott. These are some of the puzzling facts requiring explanation.

His theory of definite descriptions offers a solution to these puzzles. It consists in denying what at first blush seems obvious, namely, that sentences of the form 'the so-and-so is such-and-such' are singular in the way

'Socrates is ugly' is singular. Grammatically they are singular, but logically they are not. When their logical structure is fully analyzed they are seen to be three propositions rolled into one. Take (2) for example; the three propositions it asserts are:

(a)   There is at least one present king of France;
(b)   There is at most one present king of France;
(c)   Whoever is a present king of France is bald.

Each of these may be true (or false) independently of the others. In this example (a) is false, because France is not a monarchy. Therefore, the proposition asserted by (2) is also false, since if one conjunct of a conjunction is false, the conjunction itself is false. The puzzle about (2) and (3) has now been solved, if we read (3), as Russell thought we should, as 'it is not the case that the present king of France is bald'. Read in this way it is true. The other way of reading it, by construing 'not bald' as 'non-bald', yields a false proposition, for exactly the reason that (2) is false.

Before turning to the other puzzles, let us consider what has happened to 'the present king of France' in the analysis just outlined. Put most simply it has been dissolved by the analysis; in its place we have a predicate which we might render as 'x is a present king of France'. The uniqueness suggested by 'the' is now shared between (a) and (b). Together, if both are true, they yield a unique present king of France. The dissolution of the definite description Russell took as showing that phrases of the form 'the so-and-so' have no meaning in isolation. In order to be logical subjects of propositions they would have to have meaning in isolation, therefore they cannot be logical subjects at all. For this reason Russell called them 'incomplete symbols'. Logical analysis reveals that (2) has an unspecified subject: 'something is a present king of France and nothing else is, and that thing is bald', or, using a minimum of symbols, 'there exists an x such that x is a present king of France and, for any y, if y is a present king of France, then y is identical with x; and x is bald'. In the fully developed theory only logical notation is used, but we cannot take that step here because it presupposes a rather extensive knowledge of symbolic logic. Any standard textbook in symbolic logic can be consulted for the full analysis.

To see how the theory disposes of the puzzle about (1) we first take note of Russell's way of reading it: 'it is not the case that the golden mountain exists'. When we apply his analysis to 'the golden mountain exists' we get:

(a) There is at least one thing that is golden and a mountain;
(b) There is at most one thing that is golden and a mountain.

There is no (c) clause in the expansion of this example because 'the golden mountain exists' means the same as 'there is one and only one golden mountain', which is one way of reading the conjunction of (a) and (b). Had the example been 'the golden mountain is craggy', there would be a (c) clause. This contrast shows that 'exists' is not a predicate on the same logical level as 'craggy'. In the expansion it is clear that (a) is false, so Russell's way of reading (1) is true, which is what we expect it to be. Notice that its truth no longer obliges us to assume that the golden mountain is some kind of entity, because the analysis dissolves it into two predicates, 'x is golden' and 'x is a mountain', which may be separately true (or false) of a thing.

Turning to the perplexity generated by (4) and (5), the analysis of (4) yields:

(a) There is at least one person who wrote *Waverley*;
(b) There is at most one person who wrote *Waverley*;
(c) Whoever wrote *Waverley* is called Scott.

Here all three propositions are true, hence (4) is true. Notice that (b) would be false if *Waverley* had more than one author and (c) would be false for anyone other than Scott. Russell's analysis makes it clear why (4) is more informative than (5) and also why 'the author of *Waverley*' does not mean 'Scott'. 'The central point of the theory of descriptions was that a phrase may contribute to the meaning of a sentence without having any meaning at all in isolation. Of this, in the case of descriptions, there is precise proof: If "the author of *Waverley*" meant anything other than "Scott", "Scott is the author of *Waverley*" would be false, which it is not. If "the author of *Waverley*" meant "Scott", "Scott is the author of *Waverley*" would be a tautology, which it is not. Therefore, "the author of *Waverley*" means neither "Scott" nor anything else – i.e. "the author of *Waverley*" means nothing. Q.E.D.' (*1959*, 85).

Russell's work on definite descriptions served to warn logicians that grammatical structure is not a sure guide to logical structure. Everyone, Russell included, had formerly approached logical problems tacitly assuming that grammar was such a guide. That assumption now lay shattered. One could still begin a problem of analysis by admitting the assumption tentatively, but one had to be prepared to abandon it if the need arose. Logical analysis was made both freer and more difficult by his discovery.

V
METAPHYSICS: 'THE SKELETON OF THE WORLD'

Some of Russell's most important work in philosophy is directed to answering questions which are significant for science. If science is to be true, great care must be taken to ensure that, at the point where it touches our experience, i.e. where it is to be verified or falsified, it has been thoroughly analyzed. If, at that point, there are doubts, then the whole structure of science will be tainted with the same doubts. In physics, if the nature of physical objects is not known, then physics itself, which must rely upon physical objects to verify its theories, cannot be known. Broadly speaking, there are two ways of coming to know a thing: one is to study it directly until it discloses its secrets; the other is to construct a model which has all of the properties that the thing has. As we have seen he opted for the second way of knowing. Logical constructions are to be substituted, wherever possible, for inferred or postulated entities. Physical objects are essential to physics and minds to psychology, yet he found that neither science had analyzed the nature of these entities. By the time he was ready to turn his attention to these questions, he felt very confident of succeeding where others had failed. In October 1912, in a letter to Lady Ottoline, he exclaimed: 'I feel that I really have got a method that gives more precision than there has ever been before, and more power of getting a the skeleton of the world – the framework that things are built on.'

Physical objects were his first concern. In *Our Knowledge of the External World* he developed a model of the system of physical objects we call the world, 'which *may* be actual' (*1914*, 101). He began the construction, as he thought we must, with our common knowledge of ordinary objects, derived from personal acquaintance and the testimony of others. We are all prepared to admit that we are sometimes mistaken with regard to our detailed knowledge of a thing, but we are not prepared to admit that we are always mistaken. Philosophers have sometimes written as if we should call all of our beliefs into question at once, but this is impossible, for it leaves us without a standard by which to judge. Our knowledge has its roots in our homely beliefs; clarification, refinement, and development within the set of them is what has led to science.

Since there is no external standard to which we can appeal, we must use some of our beliefs to criticize others. This exercise will result in a relative ranking of our data, and we find we feel most certain about the things we are directly acquainted with in sense experience and less certain when testimony is involved, although we do not accord all testimony the same place on the scale, since its reliability varies.

Having made an initial sorting of our data according to its certainty, the next step is to sort it out logically. Some beliefs, those accepted on their own account, are primitive, and some, those involving inference, are derivative. An example of a primitive belief is the colour of an object to sight; an example of a derivative one is that one object is more distant than another. He did not think a sharp distinction could be drawn between these two kinds of data, for they merge into one another. Nevertheless the difference is a real one. Within the class of derivative beliefs a further distinction can be made: some are logically, and others psychologically, derivative. An example of a psychologically derivative belief is our belief that everyday objects continue to exist when we close our eyes. This belief is psychologically derivative because it depends upon our belief that we were just perceiving the objects. As far as logic goes, however, it is a primitive belief because no proof of it can be given. Such beliefs yield quickly to doubt. Because of this characteristic he thought that psychologically derivative beliefs are more in need of justification than those which are psychologically primitive, e.g. our belief that we are now seeing black marks on a white surface as we read.

His next move was to draw a distinction, vague but useful, between our hard and our soft data. Hard data resist doubt, whereas soft data tend to dissolve when subjected to doubt. Hard data are the particular facts of sense and the general truths of logic. In contrast to soft data, continued reflection upon hard data results in our being more, not less, certain of them. We can say we doubt them, but in his opinion this is a case of verbal, not genuine, doubt. Soft data are all those psychologically derivative, but logically primitive beliefs, which, as we have noted, are susceptible to doubt, In some cases we can replace their psychological derivation with a logical one; then they cease to be data but remain beliefs.

If we take only hard data, what sort of world can be constructed? To the limited store of hard data some additions can be made: some very recent facts of memory; some introspective facts; some facts of sense perception involving space and time, such as a short quick motion which we seem to see all at once; and some facts of comparison, e.g. that a grapefruit is larger than a clementine. We cannot, however, include our beliefs that objects persist, because, as we have just seen, it is psychologically derivative, or that other people have minds, because this belief arises from observation of their bodily behaviour and is therefore derivative. For the same reason we must exclude the testimony of others.

Russell was now ready to consider the problem of the external world: 'Can the existence of anything other than our own hard data be inferred from the existence of those data?' (*1914*, 80). He puts the question this way in order to exclude one natural association that the word 'external' has. To many it suggests 'spatially external', but he thought this a mistake, because, in ordinary sense experience, we are given spatial relations too. If 'external' were meant in this sense, there would be no doubt that an external world exists. In order to exclude the possibility that the use of our hard data allows those data to be caused by ourselves, as our thoughts and feelings seem to be, he recast his question: can we 'know that objects of sense, or any other objects not our own thoughts and feelings, exist at times when we are not perceiving them?' (*1914*, 82)

A question which is suggested by this one is the question concerning the thing-in-itself, or matter. Since we feel passive in sense perception, it is natural to think that our perceptions are caused by something not under our control. This belief is reinforced by noticing that similar sense impressions seem to emanate from the same place. It is further strengthened by the common tendency to attribute aberrations in sense impressions emanating from a common source to a change of conditions within ourselves or our immediate environment. These are the antecedent circumstances for the common-sensical belief in the thing-in-itself. If this is supposed to be an argument for the existence of the thing-in-itself, Russell thought it was circular. Right at the start it is assumed that the various sense impressions are appearances of the same thing. In other words the putative argument assumes there is some one thing (which is not experienced) with many appearances (which are experienced). Common sense has the matter exactly reversed from what it should be: he will take the appearances of a thing as the blocks out of which the thing itself will be constructed.

What he proposed to do is to set up a model and then test its adequacy. Limiting his discussion to sight he assumed that each mind has a view of, or perspective on, the world which is peculiar to itself. What is perceived at any given moment is a very rich three-dimensional world. Places within this world are constituted by the things in and around them; such places are not places in any other perspective because two people cannot have the very same visual experience, at best their experiences are closely similar but there will always be some differences between them. Next he assumed that each perspective exists exactly as it is perceived, and further, that it might have existed that way even if it were not perceived. An unperceived perspective may undergo changes at the moment it is perceived by someone, but he thinks that something existed at that spot before the perceiver entered it. A person who sits down between two others enjoys a perspective similar to, but not identical with, theirs; if the perspective were entirely due to the perceiver, how could one account for the similarity? He thought the simplest hypothesis was the one he favoured.

Two perspectives are spatially close together when there is a high correlation between their elements. This test requires, of course, that the perspectives be perceived; when they are, they are called 'private worlds'. The spatial relation between private worlds is not perceived by either of them, because public space, which is required here, is known only be inference. We have direct perception only of the spatial relations between things in our private world. Between any two perspectives there is a third, so public space is continuous in all its dimensions.

We are now in a position to outline the way an ordinary object is constructed out of its appearances. The first stage is to collect into a system all of its appearances at a given time; this provides the data for a logical construction of the object at that time. We may illustrate his procedure this way. Consider a lighted room bare of everything except a table. At every point, or perspective, in the room there is an appearance of the table. These appearances are first ordered into series and then the series are collected into a class. To start with, using techniques of mathematical logic, we form the various series in which shape is constant and size varies; then, by the same means, we form the various series in which size remains constant and shape varies. As we walk along what is called a line of sight toward the table we successively experience the members of one of the first sort of series; as we move around the table at a fixed distance from it we successively experience the members of one of the second sort of series. The members of the first collection of series radiate out from where we would ordinarily say the table is, like spokes from a hub; the members of the second collection of series enclose the common-sensical table in a set of partial spheres, the physical properties of the room preventing complete spheres. Once we have formed many instances of the two kinds of series they are collected together, again using techniques of mathematical logic, into one class. This constructed class *is* the momentary table.

Constructions of this kind amount to making a public space out of private spaces, because one begins by selecting a private space and then orders the other perspectives, some of which may also be private spaces, by their similarity to the one chosen. The momentary table is at the place in public space where the series which vary by size converge. In the language of common sense: the table appears larger the closer you are to it.

In finished constructions of the sort just sketched every appearance of a thing belongs to two classes. In the first place it is a member of the class of all the appearances of the thing. At most one member of this class appears in each perspective. This class is of interest to the physicist. In the second place every appearance is a member of a perspective, only some of which are perceived. Perceived perspectives are of interest to the psychologist. These two classes are associated with two places. The active place of an appearance is the place of the thing of which it is an appearance; the passive place of an appearance is the place of the perspective to which the appearance belongs. The place of a perspective in public space gives 'here' a precise meaning for each of its uses.

So far the construction yields only a momentary thing. Since things, like minds, have histories, the logical construction of a thing is a series of its momentary states, just as a mind is a series of the momentary perspectives which constitute its states. These immensely complicated collections, called 'biographies', none of which Russell ever constructed in full detail, are governed by certain laws: things by physical laws, and minds by psychological laws. For a mind to be aware of a thing means that their biographies intersect. Any appearance which appears to some mind without being a member of an intersecting biography is called 'wild'. An hallucinatory pink elephant is an example of a wild appearance.

The logical construction of the external world so far proposed does not make use of the testimony of others, because such testimony, being psychologically derivative, is classified as soft data. If a way of admitting such testimony can be found then a very much richer construction is possible. According to Russell, the only plausible argument for the existence of other minds is one by analogy. Your behaviour resembles mine; mine is accompanied by consciousness; therefore, it is likely that yours is too. The conclusion of this argument is only probable, not certain, because people in dreams also act as we do but, when we awaken, we deny to them consciousness; he saw no easy refutation of the hypothesis that all life is a dream. Descartes's evil genius cannot be exorcized, but Russell accords it a very low probability. Even though the argument from analogy is not as strong as one could wish, still there is no reason to think its conclusion false, and adopting it as a working hypothesis, which he does, brings system to much of our experience. The testimony of others can now be appealed to, so the pool of data for logical constructions is much larger and the system of private worlds, assumed above, becomes a reality.

The argument given in the last paragraph was stated in common-sensical language, and Russell often stated it that way. But when he was writing technical philosophy he usually found more general ways to state his arguments. Here is the same argument as he advanced it in *The Analysis of Matter* (1927) , his most technical book on the problem of the external world: 'Given an observed correlation among our own percepts, in which the second term is what one would naturally call a percept of our own bodily behaviour, and given a percept of similar behaviour in a physical object not our own body but similar to it, we infer that this behaviour was preceded by an event analogous to the earlier term in the observed correlation among our percepts' (206). This way of stating the argument has the added merit, he tells us, of assuming 'nothing as to the distinction of mind and body or as to the nature of either', a very important consideration in the argument of that book.

In his earlier work on logical constructions Russell favoured sense-data as his building blocks. 'Let us give the name 'sense-data' to the things that are immediately known in sensation: such things as colours, sounds, smells, hardnesses, roughnesses, and so on' (*1912*, 17). Sense-data are physical things, and appearances are complex sense-data. As the above sketch of the logical construction of the momentary table will have made clear he allowed for merely possible sense-data; these are aspects of a thing in an unperceived perspective. For a short while he used the word 'sensibile' to emphasize that his system permitted merely possible sense-data. 'I shall give the name *sensibilia* to those objects which have the same metaphysical and physical status as sense-data, without necessarily being data to any mind. Thus the relation of a *sensibile* to a sense-datum is like that of a man to a husband: a man becomes a husband by entering into the relation of marriage; and similarly a *sensibile* becomes a sense-datum by entering into the relation of acquaintance' (*1918*, 149). Both words are needed because we want a vocabulary that allows for discussion of the question whether sense-data continue to exist when no one is perceiving them. In addition to being physical both sense-data and sensibilia endure for short periods of time.

From what has been said it is apparent that both sense-data and sensibilia presuppose a subject which is, or can become, acquainted with them. His attempts to gain knowledge by acquaintance of his own self left him uneasy; his doubts about the self, or subject, grew, encouraged by the arguments of William James and his followers, that there is no such thing as consciousness. James's pure experience yields physical objects when it is organized in one way and minds when organized in another way, but the original stuff, pure experience, is neither physical nor mental. It is neutral, hence his position came to be called 'neutral monism'. For some years Russell flirted with this position without accepting it. In the 1920s he finally did accept a modified version of it, but, for his building blocks, he selected events rather than James's pure experience. 'We shall find, if I am not mistaken', he wrote in *The Analysis of Matter*, 'that the objects which are mathematically primitive in physics, such as electrons, protons, and points in space-time, are all logically complex structures composed of entities which are metaphysically more primitive, which may be conveniently called "events". It is a matter for mathematical logic to show how to construct, out of these, the objects required by the mathematical physicist.' And he goes on to the more general point: 'To show that the traditional separation between physics and psychology, mind and matter, is not metaphysically defensible, will be one of the purposes of this work; but the two will be brought together, not be subordinating either to the other, but by displaying each as a logical structure composed of what, following Dr H. M. Sheffer, we shall call "neutral stuff". We shall not contend that there are demonstrative grounds in favour of this construction, but only that it is recommended by the usual scientific grounds of economy and comprehensiveness of theoretical explanation' (9–10).

Even this short summary of his analysis of the external world will have revealed the enormous complexity of the constructions he believed required for a full understanding of physical objects. It would be a mistake to suppose that he ever intended to carry out any of these constructions fully, nor did he expect others to do so, although some did try. What he wants to show is the possibility of the constructions, and that these constructions have the properties we expect physical objects to have. Only the logical structure of the constructions interest him, because this is all we can know about the external world. The phrases, 'the skeleton of the world' and 'the framework that things are built on', which he used to convey his general idea to Lady Ottoline, are both structural notions. The notion of structure occupies a central place in *The Analysis of Matter*. In the course of summarizing his long, and at times very complex and difficult, argument he remarks: 'These principles enable us to infer a great deal as to the structure of the physical world, but not as to its intrinsic character' (400). 'As to intrinsic character, we do not know enough about it in the physical world to have a right to say that it is very different from that of percepts; while as to structure we have reason to hold that it is similar in the stimulus and the percept' (400). The causal theory of perception, which he expounds and defends in the book, provides him the assurance that there is a structural similarity between the stimulus and the percept. Percepts have causes which are not themselves percepts; when a number of people have similar percepts at the same time, a common enough occurrence, their percepts can be arranged around a central core (in the manner outlined above); using the principle, 'different effects, different causes', we infer that these percepts are like their cause in structure, while allowing that the stimulus may have structural properties not revealed in the percepts. If 'we see red and green side by side, there is some difference between the stimulus to the red percept and the stimulus to the green percept' (400). What the stimuli are in themselves we do not know, although we do know that they differ in some way, because the inverse of 'different effects, different causes' is the more familiar, 'same cause, same effect'. If the stimuli were the same, the percepts would be the same, but since they differ, the stimuli must differ in some way, even though we do not know in what the difference consists. His constructions, to repeat, reveal only the structure of physical objects and not what they are in themselves.

Given the enormous complexity of his logical constructions and the high level of logical sophistication required for any significant work on them, it is hardly surprising that only a very few took them up. Some younger philosophers during the inter-war years did attempt them, with varying degrees of success; most of them abandoned their projects when their full complexity became apparent. Those whose knowledge of logic was sufficient to the task, the leading logical positivists for example, shifted their attention to linguistic problems, and began constructing various formal languages and studying their properties. This trend dismayed Russell somewhat; he thought that many of these philosophers had forgotten that the purpose of language was to deal with non-linguistic matters. Language is used to order food in restaurants, to give directions, and so on. 'The verbalist theories of some modern philosophers forget the homely practical uses of every-day words, and lose themselves in a neo-neo Platonic mysticism. I seem to hear them saying "in the beginning was the Word", not "in the beginning was what the words means". It is remarkable that this reversion to ancient metaphysics should have occurred in the attempt to be ultra-empirical' (*1940*, 148–9). This judgment came in a book in which he too was engaged in the attempt to find answers to linguistic problems, but, as his criticism makes plain, he prided himself on not losing sight of the relation of language to the world.

VI
EPISTEMOLOGY: 'A MAP OF THE THEORY OF KNOWLEDGE'

One of the first moves Russell made in tackling the problem of the external world was to distinguish his hard data from his soft data. This was accomplished, the reader will recall, by appealing to the degree of certainty attaching to each datum. Such an exercise makes use of a notion which is central to his theory of knowledge. In that part of his philosophy he was concerned to provide a classification of kinds of knowledge, according to the degree of certainty each kind exhibits. In a letter to Lady Ottoline, written at midnight on 12 July 1911 when he was hard at work on *The Problems of Philosophy*, he remarked: 'Doing this book has given me a map of the theory of knowledge, which I hadn't before. From that point of view it will have been a great help to my own work' (#146). The organization of knowledge in that book provides a nice example of the way in which he thought epistemology should be done.

The most fundamental distinction in our knowledge concerns its object: there is knowledge of things and there is knowledge of truths. Knowledge of things is of two kinds, immediate and derivative. Immediate knowledge of things is also called 'knowledge by acquaintance'. We are acquainted with the elements comprising our sense experience, for example, when we see a red patch before us. We have knowledge by acquaintance not only of the particular elements of our experience but also of universals: that is, we are acquainted not just with a particular red patch but also with redness itself. Universals include sensible qualities like redness, and relations like 'greater than'. Error is impossible in knowledge by acquaintance.

Derivative knowledge of things is also called 'knowledge by description'. We know historical figures, for example, by description. If we claim knowledge of, say, Napoleon, our knowledge is based in part upon acquaintance, for we have seen pictures of him, and in part upon knowledge of truths, for we accept the testimony of those who were acquainted with Napoleon's appearance and who reported that he resembled the likenesses with which we are acquainted. When we come upon a descriptive statement which we do not understand, we must, if we want to understand it, research it to the point where we achieve acquaintance with the things the statement is about. In the course of our research we will make use, as we always must, of knowledge of truths. Knowledge by description, because of its partial dependence on knowledge of truths, is capable of error.

Knowledge of truths is also of two kinds, immediate and derivative. Truths known immediately are also called intuitive or self-evident truths. 'I am now seeing a white patch' is an example of this sort of truth. Some truths of logic, especially the simpler ones like 'A is A', are also instances. Our derivative knowledge of truths comprises all those truths which are deducible from intuitive truths using intuitive logical truths as our rules of inference. This fact makes intuitive truths central to his classification of knowledge.

His theory of knowledge comes to rest in intuitive, or self-evident, truths, because the process of demanding reasons for what we believe cannot go on forever. It must have an end. The process of demanding reasons can be followed until we come to truths like 'either *p* or not-*p*'. The right answer to give to one who demands a reason for the truth of this principle is that it is self-evident. For those having difficulty seeing its self-evidence he suggested providing an instance, say 'either it is snowing or it is not snowing', to aid their intuitive processes.

Amongst self-evident truths is the principle of induction. It finds its place there because no proof can be given of its truth. A first, rough statement of the principle is that the future will resemble the past. David Hume was the first to recognize that a principle of this sort is assumed in all of our reasoning concerning matters of fact. In the past certain foods have proved nourishing, therefore we eat them today. When a doubt about the truth of the principle is raised, we have to agree, Russell argued, that no proof of it is possible. Nevertheless, it is an essential premiss in scientific arguments, so it has to be admitted into any complete theory of knowledge. Since it is not a derivative truth, it will have to be classed as an immediate one. It must also be given a more precise statement; here is one of Russell's: 'The principle of induction, *prima facie*, is as follows: Let there be two kinds of events, A and B (e.g. lightning and thunder), and let many instances be known in which an event of the kind A has been quickly followed by one of the kind B, and no instances to the contrary. Then either a sufficient number of instances of this sequence, or instances of suitable kinds, will make it increasingly probable that A is always followed by *B*, and in time the probability can be made to approach certainty without limit provided the right kind and number of instances can be found' (*1927a*, 279–80).

Self-evident truths of perception are of two kinds: those asserting the existence of a datum of sense, e.g. 'there is a white patch'; and those reporting analyses of a complex datum of sense, e.g. 'that white patch is circular' or 'this is below that'. Some judgments of memory are also self-evident, especially those that are recent and vivid. Faded judgments of memory have a lower degree of self-evidence than recent and vivid ones.

The admission of degrees of self-evidence is an important characteristic of his theory of knowledge. Truths with the highest degree of self-evidence are those of perception and some (usually the simpler) logical truths. Some recent and vivid memory-judgments are nearly as high on the scale. The principle of induction, it will hardly surprise anyone, enjoys somewhat less self-evidence, and so on down the line through fainter memories and complex logical truths. The introduction of a scale of self-evidence is important because it permits him to say that a proposition has a degree of self-evidence even though it is not true, and to explain his point by calling attention to another proposition in conflict with it which has a higher degree of self-evidence. The highest degree of self-evidence does seem to be a guarantee of truth; lower degrees lead only to a presumption of truth.

Since self-evidence is not always a guarantee of truth, a theory of truth is required to round out his account of our knowledge of truths. Knowledge of truths has as its opposite error, for it is possible to hold false beliefs.

He assumed that people want to avoid, if they can, false beliefs, but to do so they have to know, as a first step, the meaning of 'true' and 'false'. Any acceptable theory of the meaning of these terms must meet certain conditions: it must allow instances of both true and false beliefs; it must make 'true' and 'false' predicates of beliefs and statements; and it must require the truth or falsity of a belief to depend upon something external to the belief itself.

The third of these conditions committed him to the correspondence theory of truth. Truth consists in correspondence to fact, and falsity in the absence of such correspondence. Thus runs the basic idea of the theory. Fuller statement of it proved a good deal more difficult than a consideration of the basic idea would suggest. As a first step the theory requires that propositions point to something other than themselves; in his theory propositions have objective reference, which is a function of the meanings of the words making them up. Propositions come in pairs, since every proposition can be denied. Both a proposition and its denial have the same objective, which is a fact, but they differ in their objective references because one of them points towards the fact and the other away from it. This is because there are true and false propositions, but not true and false facts. To remove the need to know whether a proposition is true or false before its objective reference can be determined, he proposed a definition of 'the meaning of a proposition'. 'The 'meaning' of the proposition 'today is Tuesday' consists in pointing to the fact 'today is Tuesday' if it is a fact, or away from the fact 'today is not Tuesday' if that is a fact. The 'meaning' of the proposition 'today is not Tuesday' will be exactly the opposite. By this hypothetical form we are able to speak of the meaning of a proposition without knowing whether it is true or false' (*1921*, 273). On this analysis we know what would make a proposition true or false when we know what it means.

To define truth and falsity a formal statement 'of the fact that a proposition is true when it points towards its objective, and false when it points away from it' (*1921*, 273) is required. For some simple cases the correspondence is direct 'the blue pen is to the left of the yellow pencil' is verified by inspection. But what of negative propositions? Are we required to espouse the negative fact that there is no milk in the refrigerator when the corresponding proposition is true? As is plain from his definition of 'the meaning of a proposition', he thought we do have to admit negative facts. This admission seemed to many of his critics an abandonment of Occam's Razor, but he was persuaded, even after examining his critics's arguments, that negative facts have to be admitted to provide objectives for true negative propositions. The only alternative seemed to be the abandonment of the correspondence theory itself.

Relational statements like 'Henry VIII precedes Elizabeth I' do not present additional problems for the theory. In this example the relation meant by 'precedes' is put between the two names in the order given; if there is a fact of that form then the proposition is true, otherwise it is false. He felt confident that any relational proposition however complicated can be handled in the same way.

It will be plain from this brief statement of his theory that it meets the three conditions that any acceptable theory of the meaning of 'true' and 'false' must meet which were mentioned earlier. His theory also suggests the tests which our beliefs must pass to be regarded as true. Some test is required in his theory of knowledge, because, as we have seen, self-evident beliefs are sometimes in conflict; asking which of the conflicting beliefs corresponds to the facts will often resolve the conflict. Our knowledge of truths increases with each successful application of the test.

Shortly after writing *The Problems of Philosophy*, and while it was still going through the press, he paused, in a letter to Lady Ottoline of 13 December 1911, to reflect upon what he had learnt about theory of knowledge in the course of his work on it:

> There is one great question: Can human beings *know* anything, and if so what and how? This question is really the most essentially philosophical of all questions. But ultimately one has to come down to a sheer assertion that one does know this or that – e.g. one's own existence – and then one can ask why one knows it, and whether anything else fulfils the same conditions. But what is important in this inquiry can, I think, be done quite popularly; the technical refinements add very little except controversy and long words. I was reinforced in this view by finding how much I could say on the question in the shilling shocker. (#286.)

'The shilling shocker' was his pet name for *Problems*, reflecting both its selling price and also its intended readers, which were people who had been denied a higher education but were determined to pursue learning on their own – the 'students' of the Home University Library. Two years later, Russell did attempt to supply 'the technical refinements' to his theory of knowledge in a book of that name, but he made the mistake of showing his manuscript to Wittgenstein, who attacked it savagely. Russell abandoned his manuscript, but rescued some of what he wanted to say in *Our Knowledge of the External World*, which was written during September and October of 1913, only weeks after he stopped work on his earlier book.

The positions we have outlined in this chapter bear the marks of his method. No matter what philosophical problem he was concerned with, he always focused on its logic. Logic enters in two ways. There is first the question of logical priority: the logically primitive must be distinguished from the logically derivative. When that has been done, there is the question of logical structure. This is the constructive part of the work. Logical principles must be found which will bind the parts into a whole. Here he had an enormous advantage over most people because of his work on *Principia Mathematica*. That book, which also sorted the primitive from the derivative and gave derivations of all the derivative propositions, was ever after his model of what excellent philosophical work should be. His last philosophical book, *Human Knowledge, its Scope and Limits*, which studies the nature of non-demonstrative inference, shows clear marks of this model. In non-demonstrative inference the conclusion does not follow certainly, given the truth of the premises, but only with some degree of probability. Such inferences are common in science and daily life, so it is important to know to what extent they can be trusted. In his earlier work on theory of knowledge he argued for the self-evidence of the principle of induction; in this new work he took a fresh look at the problem and found that five postulates, none of which is similar in statement to his earlier principle (but which together do the work of the earlier principle) are required to validate non-demonstrative inferences. Using these postulates, which he stated and defended, he gave an elaborate argument to show that we can trust the conclusions reached by application of scientific method; the trust, of course, is a hostage to the truth of the five postulates, which rests in the final analysis on something like self-evidence.

Another observation on his model of philosophic inquiry is perhaps worth making. It seems likely that he hit upon it and came to appreciate its value when he was writing *A Critical Exposition of the Philosophy of Leibniz* (1900). In that book he argued for a new conception of Leibniz's philosophy as being deductive consequences of a few, mainly logical principles. He stated the five principles he maintained were logically primitive; he cited passages in Leibniz's writings to show that Leibniz used these principles in his philosophical thinking; and he showed how the theory of monads followed from these five premisses. In the preface to his book Russell reported that this new conception occurred to him while he was studying Leibniz's books and letters. 'I saw how its foundations were laid, and how its superstructure rose out of them. It appeared that this seemingly fantastic system could be deduced from a few simple premisses, which, but for the conclusions which Leibniz had drawn from them, many, if not most, philosophers would have been willing to admit' (*1900*, viii). Leibniz, he charged, had been too anxious to curry favour with those in positions of power and influence to lay his philosophy out in a truly orderly and systematic way. Russell does not conceal his moral indignation at this failure on Leibniz's part. His tone lets the reader know that the young Russell had resolved never to be guilty of Leibniz's sin.

VII
ETHICS: THE GROUND FOR MORAL RULES

While Russell was still living with his grandmother, before he had gone up to Cambridge, he decided that it was 'obvious that the happiness of mankind should be the aim of all action' (*1967a*, 44; *1967b*, 53), but to his intense surprise he soon discovered that not everyone agreed with this conclusion. Amongst those who scorned it most ferociously was his grandmother, who heaped ridicule on him after he made the mistake of telling her of his conversion to utilitarianism. A vindictive sort of woman, she lost few opportunities henceforth of presenting him with ethical puzzles and demanding that he solve them using utilitarian principles. What he tells us he learned from this behaviour was that she had no intellectual reasons for her opposition to utilitarianism, she simply disliked it. Her anti-intellectualism made it impossible for him to converse with her about his most important interests. Despite repeated attempts, she did not succeed in weaning him from utilitarianism. That task was performed by his friend and colleague, G. E. Moore, after he had gone up to Cambridge.

It may surprise the reader to learn that Russell's first work in ethics was undertaken as something of an assignment. In 1905 a group of young men, fired with enthusiasm for Moore's *Principia Ethica*, proposed a joint volume, a 'manifesto' they called it, in which various philosophical topics would be treated in Moore's manner. Moore himself was assigned 'truth' and Russell 'ethics'; others were to write on the remaining topics. Russell dutifully wrote his paper and sent it off to Moore, who did not like it. It is hard now to imagine why such a volume should contain a chapter on 'ethics', since the founders of the group seemed to think that Moore's book was the last word on the subject; and it is even harder to imagine why they assigned the topic to Russell, instead of to Moore. As might be expected the project fell through, so a few years later Russell sent his piece to a journal for publication in parts. Most of it did appear before the journal went bankrupt, and Russell included the entire essay in *Philosophical Essays* (1910).

In 'The Elements of Ethics' Russell hews faithfully to Moore's position. 'Good' is treated as unique and indefinable for the same reasons that Moore gives. No proposed definition of 'good', such as 'good' means 'desired' or 'good' means 'obedience to the will of God', is defensible, because it is always significant to ask, say, 'is what is desired good?', which it would not be if the original definition was a good one. Indeed, the answer to this question is sometimes 'no', which underscores both the question's significance and the failure of the proposed definition. After a lengthy discussion of the definability of 'good' Russell draws this conclusion: 'Thus *good* and *bad* are qualities which belong to objects independently of our opinions, just as much as *round* and *square* do; and when two people differ as to whether a thing is good, only one of them can be right, though it may be very hard to know which is right'

The core of his scientific method in philosophy is the analysis of propositions. In defending his method he had to answer two charges laid against analysis as a method. The first was a very old one: namely, that analysis, by its very nature, leads to falsification. In *The Principles of Mathematics*, his first large work using the analytic method, he discussed this charge:

> I have already touched on a very important logical doctrine, which the theory of whole and part brings into prominence – I mean the doctrine that analysis is falsification. Whatever can be analyzed is a whole, and we have already seen that analysis of wholes is in some measure falsification. But it is important to realize the very narrow limits of this doctrine. We cannot conclude that the parts of a whole are not really its parts, nor that the parts are not presupposed in the whole in a sense in which the whole is not presupposed in the parts, nor yet that the logically prior is not usually simpler than the logically subsequent. In short, though analysis gives us the truth, and nothing but the truth, yet it can never give us the whole truth. This is the only sense in which the doctrine is to be accepted. In any wider sense, it becomes merely a cloak for laziness, by giving an excuse to those who dislike the labour of analysis. (*1903*, 141.)

Towards the end of his book he comes back to this point. In discussing the then prevalent notion that things were 'organic unities, composed of many parts expressing the whole and expressed in the whole', he argues that there are no such 'organic unities'. 'In every case of analysis, there is a whole consisting of parts with relations; it is only the nature of the parts and the relations which distinguishes different cases. Thus the notion of an organic whole in the above sense must be attributed to defective analysis, and cannot be used to explain things' (466). Taking up explicitly the charge that analysis is falsification – that the complex arrived at through analysis is not equivalent to what one began with – since what gives it unity has been lost, Russell agrees that this is true whenever what is analyzed is a unity. 'A proposition has a certain indefinable unity, in virtue of which it is an assertion; and this is so completely lost by analysis that no enumeration of constituents will restore it, even though itself be mentioned as a constituent. There is, it must be confessed, a grave logical difficulty in this fact, for it is difficult not to believe that a whole must be constituted by its constituents. For us, however, it is sufficient to observe that all unities are propositions or propositional concepts, and that consequently nothing that exists is a unity. If, therefore, it is maintained that things are unities, we must reply that no things exist' (466–7). In his subsequent work, especially in *Theory of Knowledge* (written in 1913 but not published until 1984), Russell has no further discussion of this ancient charge. A string of successes in analyzing propositions, culminating in the system of *Principia Mathematica*, seemed to undermine the importance of it. But what he had seen as 'a grave logical difficulty' was to return to haunt him when Wittgenstein criticized his theory of judgment in *Theory of Knowledge* as defective, in part because the unity of a judgment was not preserved in his analysis; and by breaking off his work on the book, Russell seems, at the time at least, to have agreed with Wittgenstein. But, as we have seen, he was to resume use of his method a few years later and continue to use it the rest of his life. Whatever its deficiency in this respect, it was, in his opinion, the best available method.

matters not dignified in themselves but important for their consequences, as the man of science does with his test-tubes; how the love of system, since new facts are the enemies of systems, has to be kept rigidly in check, in spite of being a thing every philosopher ought to have; how vital it is to avoid emotion and edification and the wish to be literary. Some day I must write on how to study philosophy; I have a lot to say about it. There is so much to be found out by patience and a scientific spirit. ... Geach asked me if I thought him too much of a disciple, so I said I did, and that led me on to say how I didn't want to teach a doctrine, but a spirit, an attitude to philosophy. I do care *enormously* about that.

This striking passage seems to me to epitomize both his conception of philosophy and his ideas of how it should be taught.

Russell was convinced that his method had two important considerations in its favour. In the first place, it can be used to solve certain problems once and (with suitable later refinement) for all. Such problems are of limited scope, and they are likely to be subsidiary aspects of a greater problem, but this does not matter because their solution, if it can be found, gives one a definite hold on the larger problem. Adjustments will be required in the earlier hypotheses once the larger problem is tackled, but this is just what a person of scientific temperament expects. Russell's solutions to problems are offered in a tentative way, as the best he has been able to come up with. Progress in science is piecemeal; only at a very late stage is a solution to the whole problem advanced. And he believed the same was true of philosophy. In the second place, this method opens the way for cooperative work in philosophy. Large problems can be worked upon at the same time by a number of researchers, who circulate partial results among their fellow workers for criticism and for whatever use others may make of them. In this way problems that are too big for one person can perhaps be solved.

Philosophy, according to this view, is just one more science, neither better nor worse than the others. This view, it hardly need be said, was at variance with the positions taken by most of his contemporaries in philosophy. Many, and here the then dominant idealistic school is included, wrote as if philosophy was a much grander subject than mere science, when they condescended to take notice of science at all. Others, Herbert Spencer and Henri Bergson are his prime examples, thought that philosophers should take scientific results and erect a philosophy on them. Russell's reply to the first group has already been given; he thought there was no separate method for philosophy, so they were simply mistaken. The second group were wrong for two reasons: first, because at any given time scientific results are based on a small selection from all possible experience, and hence the manner of selection may be as relevant as the data selected; and second, because all scientific results, and especially the most general of them, are constantly being corrected, with the result that taking them as a basis for philosophical generalization at some particular time is to treat them as no longer corrigible, which is a grave error. A philosophy based on scientific generalizations will find itself swept away when those generalizations require correction, as is bound to happen sooner or later.

If philosophy is just one more science, how is it to be distinguished from its sister sciences? To the extent it can be distinguished Russell thought it was by two

(*1992*, 223). Russell here recognizes one of the persistent difficulties of the Moorean position, namely, how are disagreements to be settled when one person says 'A is good' and another says 'A is bad'? It hardly seems right for one of them to accuse the other of moral blindness, but when all that can be said has been said, and no mind has been changed, what other course is open? The answer is not obvious. George Santayana, as we will see below, set his sights on just this point.

Taking it as established that some things are intrinsically good and others intrinsically bad, Russell turns to an analysis of the notion of 'right'. 'Right' and 'wrong', which apply to actions, are not fundamental notions in ethics, that honour goes to 'good' and 'bad'. It is, therefore, in terms of their effects, that actions are judged to be 'right' or 'wrong'. An action is right in a certain situation, if its 'probable effects are, on the whole, better than those of any other action which is possible under the circumstances' (234). The effects, of course, are examined for their intrinsic goodness (or badness). The word 'possible' is freighted with meaning in this statement; not only must the action be physically possible for the person contemplating it to perform, but it must also be one that it is possible for that person to have thought of in the time leading up to doing it, and it must be one that it is possible for that person to choose if he or she does happen to think of it. Since capacity for thought varies greatly, Russell distinguishes between actions that are 'objectively right' and those that are 'morally right':

> The *objectively right* action, in any circumstances, is that action which, of all that are possible, gives us, when account is taken of all available data, the greatest expectation of probable good effects, or the least expectation of

probable bad effects. The *subjectively right* or *moral* action is that one which will be judged by the agent to be objectively right if he devotes to the question an appropriate amount of candid thought, or, in the case of actions that ought to be impulsive, a small amount. The appropriate amount of thought depends upon the importance of the action and the difficulty of the decision. (235.)

Both sorts of actions, of course, also presuppose that the agent is capable of discerning the intrinsic value of the effects. Such a highly intellectualized ethic would seem to be beyond the capacity of most people, but it was very attractive to many young people around Cambridge in the first decade of this century. And for a short period Russell claimed it as his own.

'The Elements of Ethics' contains much detailed argument in support of this position. The theory of determinism, which requires that all actions be caused, is shown to be compatible with it. Many people have a prejudice against determinism and assert a belief in free-will, which upon examination seems to be the doctrine that some (perhaps only a tiny) part of the causes of a person's actions are spontaneous, uncaused acts of will. Russell argues that those who profess to hold the doctrine of free-will are muddled in their thinking. Such people do not refrain from seeking to get others to act differently, but, when they do, their behaviour presupposes that they know the sort of causes that produce actions and they believe that calling attention to these causes will prove effective. 'People never do, as a matter of fact, believe that any one else's actions are not determined by motives, however much they may think *themselves* free' (238–9). Earlier he explained that by 'motive' he means 'a cause of volition'.

Egoism, or the view that a person's first duty is to herself, does not, he argues, make it impossible for one to perform objectively right actions. The argument turns on analyzing the meaning of 'my good'; a long, detailed, and intricate critique of the two most promising senses of the phrase convinces Russell that there is no form of egoism which is defensible. In addition to the argument from analysis, there is an appeal to facts: a candid and searching examination of human actions and desires, with no theory in mind, shows 'that most of them are objective and have no direct reference to self' (242). Here again people commonly deceive themselves by paying too little attention to the language in which they express themselves. Even people who explicitly deny that there is a common good use language in such a way as to show they do believe there is a common good. 'Everybody judges that some sorts of communities are better than others; and most people who affirm that when they say a thing is good they mean merely that they desire it, would admit that it is better two people's desires should be satisfied than only one person's' (243). In this way they pass, without perhaps realizing it, from the conception of 'my good' or 'your good' to simply 'good'. He concludes that 'we ought to pursue the general good, and when this conflicts with self-interest, self-interest ought to give way' (245).

At the end of his essay he returns to the question of what is good and what is bad intrinsically. No list is given on the ground that 'the reader is probably quite as capable as I am of judging what things are good and what bad' (245). His concern is to refute an ethical scepticism which holds that it is a waste of time to try to achieve agreement on values. With the possible exception of immediate and simultaneous judgments of value, when one person applies 'good' and the other 'bad', Russell thinks that most disagreements about the value of a thing or state of affairs are amenable to argument. Two common errors are those of the philosopher, who loves system and who distorts individual judgments to fit the system, and those of the moralist, who puts an undue emphasis upon means and, as a consequence, frequently loses sight of ends, which are, after all, the things that are intrinsically good or bad. Judgments of value with the best chance of wide agreement are those made by persons who avoid both these errors; immediate inspection of the ends to be judged is the best way to secure wide agreement. A further complication arises when the judgment to be made is of something which is part of a greater whole, which itself must be assigned a value. These 'organic unities' (248), as he calls them, present the most difficult challenges, but, even in judging these, he is sanguine on the prospects for agreement, if people will only use their heads and avoid the mistakes he has warned against. 'The making of such judgments we did not undertake; for if the reader agrees, he could make them himself, and if he disagrees without falling into any of the possible confusions, there is no way of altering his opinion' (250). Moore did not like Russell's final section, and urged that it be omitted; it may have been because Russell has laid out too plainly one of the worst weaknesses of this sort of ethic.

When Russell next writes about ethics he takes quite a different line. 'On Scientific Method in Philosophy' seems an unlikely place to find such a discussion, but the question of ethical notions must be faced, because so much of traditional philosophy involves them. Such notions are essentially anthropocentric and consequently, whenever they are appealed to, import into the discussion the present desires of human beings, thus distorting the 'receptivity to fact which is the essence of the scientific attitude towards the world' (*1918*, 107). All ethics in his opinion is subjective: 'Ethics is in origin the art of recommending to others the sacrifices required for co-operation with oneself. Hence, by reflexion, it comes, through the operation of social justice, to recommend sacrifices by oneself, but all ethics, however refined, remains more or less subjective' (108). It is because human beings are gregarious that they produce an ethic, acting on their instinct to conduct themselves in harmony with those in their own group, while opposing those in other groups. 'Those who belong to our own group are good; those who belong to hostile groups are wicked' (108). The fact that its principles apply to all members of the group lulls its members into regarding these principles as objective, when any outsider could set them right, but outsiders are seldom attended to. This analysis is able to account for such an ethical notion as self-sacrifice, because it is sometimes demanded of a member for the good of the group. Circumstances in which this happens give rise to a conflict between the instinct of the individual to preserve itself and the desire of that same individual to do what is for the good of the whole group. Self-sacrifice occurs in circumstances where the desire proves stronger than the instinct. Since ethical notions are essentially subjective, they fall outside the purview of scientific philosophy. For the rest of his life, although he sometimes discussed ethical concepts at length, he almost invariably prefaced such discussions with the disclaimer that he was not engaged in philosophy at such times.

This sketch of an ethic, and it is no more than a sketch, is so diametrically opposed to the doctrines set forth at such length in 'The Elements of Ethics' that we have to wonder what happened in the space of five years to persuade him to abandon an objective ethic for a subjective one. In *An Outline of Philosophy* (1927) he wrote that his change of mind was 'partly' (230) due to the criticisms George Santayana had made of the earlier essay in an article published shortly after *Philosophical Essays* came out.

Santayana's criticisms, in a book with the wonderful title *Winds of Doctrine*, are, it must be admitted, devastating; he takes Russell and Moore severely to task for hypostatizing 'good', and he supports his case with exceptional force. Here is a sample of his argument:

> For the human system whiskey is truly more intoxicating than coffee, and the contrary opinion would be an error; but what a strange way of vindicating this real, though relative, distinction, to insist that whiskey is more intoxicating in itself, without reference to any animal; that it is pervaded, as it were, by an inherent intoxication, and stands dead drunk in its bottle! Yet just in this way Mr Russell and Mr Moore conceive things to be dead good and dead bad. It is such a view, rather than a naturalistic one, that renders reasoning and self-criticism impossible in morals; for wrong desires, and false opinions as to value, are conceivable only because a point of reference or criterion is available to prove them such. If no point of reference and no criterion were admitted to be relevant, nothing but physical stress could give to one assertion of value greater force than to another. The shouting moralist no doubt has his place, but not in philosophy. (*1913*, 146–7.)

Having exploded Russell's central doctrine, that 'good' is a quality like 'round', Santayana goes on to demolish the arguments that depend upon it. Little remains of the position when he is through. Since Russell says that he found the criticisms unanswerable, it would seem that Santayana's critique would constitute the whole of Russell's reason for abandoning an objective ethic, but, as we have noted, he says it was only part of it.

The unexpressed part of his reason may have to do with the essential nature of the earlier essay; it was, after all, undertaken as part of a joint enterprise, and his assignment was to write up Moore's ethical position for that book. There is then a certain discernible detachment in the essay; he makes the best case he can, but occasionally the reader senses that he is aware of Moore looking over his shoulder. Santayana too noticed that Russell was of two minds at certain points: 'That good in not an intrinsic or primary quality, but relative and adventitious, is clearly betrayed by Mr Russell's own way of arguing, whenever he approaches some concrete ethical question. For instance, to show that the good is not pleasure, he can avowedly do nothing but appeal 'to ethical judgments with which almost every one would agree' (*1913*, 147). Had Santayana never criticized this theory, Russell would still almost certainly have abandoned it. Santayana's critique simply accelerated matters. Indeed, in a note published in 1952, Russell said that shortly after 'Elements' was published, he came to disagree with the theory in it. 'I do not now think that "good" is undefinable, and I think that whatever objectivity the concept may possess is political rather than logical' (*1992*, 213). Reflecting on Santayana's critique, while at the same time trying to devise a new method for philosophy, seems to have led him to these conclusions.

In *An Outline of Philosophy* he devotes a chapter to ethics solely on the ground that it is a traditional part of philosophy. 'As a provisional definition, we may take ethics to consist of general principles which help to determine rules of conduct' (225). 'Ethics' must be distinguished both from 'casuistry', which is concerned with the way in which a person should behave in particular circumstances, and 'morals', which is concerned to establish actual rules of conduct. Ethics provides the ground from which moral rules are deduced. Russell makes these distinctions in order to focus his discussion, which is confined to ethics. Throughout his discussion the subjectivity of ethics is assumed established.

Taking the meaning of 'ought' as his starting place, he notes that the meaning of a sentence like, 'I ought to do so and so', is primarily emotional; it means that towards the act described by 'so and so' I have an emotion of approval. But no one wants such an ephemeral ethic; 'we want to find something more objective and systematic and constant than a personal emotion' (226) to support our claim that this is what we ought to do. The next step is then to find reasons for accepting the claim that anyone ought to approve such an action. History helps here. One traditional reason is obedience to authority. Those who obey authority are virtuous; those who disobey are punished. In some cases the authority is embodied in a set of commandments, which are supposed to serve as a guide in all situations. A great defect of a set of command-ments, as history shows, is that they cannot possibly anticipate every situation where guidance is required, so two ethics grow up side by side. One of them decides cases by appeal to the rules, the other by appeal to the consequences of acting in one way rather than another. Such a bifurcation is unacceptable to the philosopher. Another defect of an authoritarian ethic arises out of the first; those who try to use it, find themselves, in situations falling outside the rules, evaluating consequences as desirable or undesirable in order to decide what to do. This way of evaluating is then almost unconsciously carried over to the rule-based side of ethics, and people notice that sometimes acting according to rule leads to undesirable consequences, which tends to undermine the rules. A third defect is revealed when it is asked how the moral rules are known. One of two answers is usually given: by revelation or by tradition. No philosopher, Russell thinks, can accept these grounds, because both revelation and tradition vary with different groups. How is one to pick one from the many? There can be no defensible reason for a choice, including an appeal to individual conscience, because it too varies with circumstances.

One other type of authoritarian ethic, what he calls an 'administrator's ethic', is briefly considered: here the cardinal rule is that one should obey the moral code of the group or community to which one belongs. Its fatal defect is that it makes 'it impossible to apply ethical predicates to authority: we cannot find any meaning for the statement that a custom is good or that the government is bad' (229). Such an ethic is fit only for despots and their willing slaves.

To be defensible an ethic must provide that conduct be judged by its consequences. The utilitarianism of his youth does make consequences central to its theory, but

Russell thinks happiness is not an adequate analysis of 'good', as utilitarians claim it is; such an analysis, he implies, would be too narrow. In espousing a consequentialist theory Russell wants it clearly understood that he is not saying that prior to each and every action a person must weigh the consequences of the various alternatives, instead, he reminds us that an ethic serves as the ground for a code of morals, and what he is recommending is that the decision whether or not to adopt a certain moral rule should be decided by its likely consequences. If we proceed in this way, we can bring the code up to date from time to time by re-examining it, in the light of our experience with it and in terms of its likely consequences. In this theory 'right conduct' means 'conduct calculated to produce desirable results' (230). But in order to decide which ends are desirable, we must define 'good'.

At this point in his argument Russell rejects the Moorean view that 'good' is indefinable and opts instead for an analysis in terms of 'desire'. But 'good' cannot mean 'what is desired', because desires conflict in all sorts of ways, and since language is social, the meaning of 'good' must itself be social. Russell relies heavily on the social nature of language to arrive at the conclusion that 'good' comes to apply to things desired by the whole of a social group. It is evident, therefore, that there can be more good in a world where the desires of different individuals harmonize than in one where they conflict. The supreme moral rule should, therefore, be: *Act so as to produce harmonious rather than discordant desires*' (234). Russell draws some of its consequences. It follows: that love is better than hate, because love permits the satisfaction of all parties but hate of only some; that the desire for knowledge is better than many other ends, providing it is not knowledge of how to kill others in war; and that desire for power over others is bad because it directly conflicts with the rule. His ethic can be summed up this way: *'The good life is one inspired by love and guided by knowledge'* (235).

In later years Russell discussed ethical questions twice more. In *Religion and Science* (1935) he recapitulated his theory in a chapter on 'Science and Ethics', emphasizing that ethics, because of its subjective character, falls outside science, and, indeed, because its central terms are to be defined in terms of 'desire', outside the domain of knowledge. Although it is important for human affairs, it is not a branch of knowledge. If our desires change, our values will change too; but this conflicts with the objective demands of knowledge.

> When a man says, 'This is good in itself', he *seems* to be making a statement, just as much as if he said, 'This is square' or 'This is sweet'. I believe this to be a mistake. I think that what the man really means is: 'I wish everybody to desire this', or rather, 'Would that everybody desired this'. If what he says is interpreted as a statement, it is merely an affirmation of his own personal wish; if, on the other hand, it is interpreted in a general way, it states nothing, but merely desires something. The wish, as an occurrence, is personal, but what it desires is universal. It is, I think, this curious interlocking of the particular and the universal which has caused so much confusion in ethics. (235–6.)

We see in this passage one of the central ideas of the emotive theory of ethics, later developed by Charles Stevenson.

Russell last wrote about ethics in *Human Society in Ethics and Politics* (1954). His theory remains basically that which he expounded in *An Outline of Philosophy*, although it is discussed at greater length and, consequently, is more fully developed. In an effort to make more precise his notion of 'harmonious desires' he borrows from Leibniz the idea of 'compossibility': 'I call a number of desires "compossible" when all can be satisfied by the same state of affairs; when they are not compossible, I call them incompatible' (*1954, 59*) This concept permits him, as did his definitions in logic, to state his views much more succinctly than in the earlier book. 'It is obvious that there can be a greater total of satisfaction of desire where desires are compossible than where they are incompatible' (*59*). Since 'good' means 'the satisfaction of desire', the latter phrase can be replaced by 'good' in this sentence. 'Right' can also be defined in terms of 'compossibility'. Aside from refinements of the language in which it is expressed, his basic theory remains unchanged.

It is clear that his ethic puts a heavy responsibility on educational institutions, because it is only by means of education that individuals can be made to see that it is better to opt for those actions which maximize the satisfaction of desires of all those affected by the action. Thus, this ethical theory fits much better than the Moorean one with the principle of growth, which as we will see, is central to his view of human nature, and, hence, to his political theory. But it may put an unbearable burden upon the schools; the sorts of calculation involved would seem to be beyond the ken of most people, who want the security of a set of rules by which to guide their action. Russell would probably reply that his theory can be used to establish such a set of rules, but he would also be quick to warn us that it would be necessary periodically to ensure that the code was up to date, by examining it in the light of the accumulated experience of its use. He was ever sanguine about the ability of humans to reform themselves.

VIII
RELIGION: A SCEPTIC'S TESTAMENT

From time to time throughout his career Russell turned
his attention to traditional questions in the philosophy
of religion. To them, as to more purely philosophical
problems, he applied the methods of analysis honed
during his years of work on logic. On the question of
the existence of God, there are several well-known
arguments which purport to prove His existence. What
is perhaps the most respectable of them, the ontological
argument, can be stated in several ways, but all of the
ways have as their nerve the claim that the divine
essence includes existence as one of its properties. The
usual way of arguing is to ask a person to contemplate
what God is in order to see that He must be, because a
perfect existent being is better than a perfect
non-existent one. In criticism of the argument, Russell
pointed out that 'God' is not a logically proper name,
although it appears to be one, because to be a proper
name in the sense demanded requires that we be
acquainted with the thing named, which no philosopher
is prepared to claim in this case. If we were acquainted
with God, we would have no need to invent arguments
to prove His existence. 'God', Russell maintained, is a
disguised definite description; 'the perfect being', as
expositions of the ontological argument make clear, is
the description usually intended. But if in a statement
of the argument we substitute 'the perfect being is

87

omniscient' for 'God is omniscient' we see at once, according to the theory of descriptions, that the question at issue – God's existence – is being begged in the argument, because the expansion of 'the perfect being is omniscient' demands, as its first clause, 'there is at least one perfect being' (*Cf. 1957, 54*). Kant rejected the ontological argument, giving as his reason that existence is not a predicate. Russell's reason for rejecting it is similar: 'existence' is not a predicate on the same logical level as 'omniscient' and 'all-good'; it is, if we want to call it a predicate at all, a predicate of predicates, or a second-order predicate. In Russell's philosophy, because of the theory of types, it may also be higher than second-order, depending upon the order of the predicate of which it is asserted. 'Exists', when a second-order predicate, is used to affirm that first-order predicates like 'red' or 'wise' have at least one instance.

The cosmological, or first cause, argument is, in Russell's opinion, formally invalid. From two premisses – (1) that something exists and (2) that whatever exists must have a cause of its existence – the conclusion is drawn that a necessary being exists. The crux of the argument is to build up a causal chain of beings that might not have existed (contingent beings) and then claim that, unless the chain comes to an end in a being which is self-caused (a necessary being), none of the contingent beings can be said to be caused, in violation of the second premiss. Russell noted that since 'something exists' is a contingent truth, the conclusion of the argument cannot both be deduced from it (and the second premiss) and also be a necessary truth, for only a contingent conclusion follows from contingent premisses (unless the premisses contradict one another, but in that case the argument is unsound).

Advocates of the argument must then believe the argument proceeds differently, since they believe it establishes its conclusion. Their only recourse is to claim that the conclusion of the argument is presupposed in the premiss that something exists, in other words, that contingent existence presupposes necessary existence. Russell agreed that if A presupposes B, then if A is true, B must be true, but he denied, what its advocates maintained, that grounds can be found to support the truth of A which are not also grounds in support of B. 'In Euclid, for example, if you admit the propositions, you must also admit the axioms; but it would be absurd to give this as a reason for admitting the axioms. Such an argument is at best *ad hominem*, when your opponent is a weak reasoner. If people are willing to admit finite existence, then you force them to admit God's existence; but if they ask a reason why they should admit finite existence, the only grounds, if the cosmological argument be valid, are such as lead first to the existence of God; such grounds, however, if they exist, are only found in the ontological argument' (*1900*, 175). We have already seen that he thought the ontological argument defective, so the required support is not forthcoming.

Two other arguments for God's existence can be dealt with more briefly. The argument from design was replaced, he believed, by the theory of evolution. This argument proceeds by analogy: men design machines; the universe resembles a machine, therefore it is probable that the universe was designed by an intelligence similar to, but proportionally greater than, human intelligence. The difference of degree between the divine and human intelligences is suggested by comparing the complexity of the universe to, say, that of the space shuttle. In his discussion of this argument Russell observed that, before Darwin, it offered an account of the adaptation of living things to their environment; but Darwin has shown that, rather than the environment having been adapted to living things, the exact reverse is true, those species which survive, survive because they have adapted to their environment. 'There is', Russell wryly noted, 'no evidence of design about it' (1957, 6).

The arguments about which he was most scornful are the so-called moral arguments for the existence of God. An example of this sort of argument is the argument for the remedying of injustice invented by Kant. This life exhibits much injustice, the argument runs, therefore there must be a God, an afterlife, and a Heaven and Hell, where justice triumphs and the wicked, who escaped justice on earth, are punished. Russell agreed with the truth of the premiss, but contended that anyone of a scientific temper of mind would draw the tentative conclusion that probably there is injustice throughout the universe. 'Supposing you got a crate of oranges that you opened, and you found all the top layer of oranges bad, you would not argue: "The underneath ones must be good, so as to redress the balance." You would say: "Probably the whole lot is a bad consignment"; and that is really what a scientific person would argue about the universe' (1957, 9).

His position on the existence of God is that of the agnostic. He knew of no argument which establishes either the existence or the non-existence of a deity. Nor did he know of any set of unexplained facts for which the hypothesis that God exists constitutes the best explanation. Therefore the hypothesis is unnecessary, although it is not known to be false.

On the question of life after death his mature philosophy gives a definite answer. To be plausible immortality required a soul, or an ego, or at least a subject, which was at the centre of a person's experience and persisted through time. There had also to be a certain degree of independence between the soul and the body, else the soul would be involved in the body's decay after death. In *The Problems of Philosophy* he was inclined to the view that the self is 'the same today as yesterday', only that 'it does seem as though we must be acquainted with that thing, whatever its nature, which sees the sun and has acquaintance with sense-data' (*1912*, 80). So even at this early date his philosophy admits only a (perhaps constantly changing) subject, and then only because his theory of perception demands it. In *The Analysis of Mind* he offered a sketch of the subject, constructed by logical means out of what are commonly called its (the subject's) experiences, which are bound together by certain causal laws, the ones which psychologists study. The subject has become a logical construction or a logical fiction; it is no longer necessary to assume its existence. The series of events which takes its place has all the properties which the subject is supposed to have, and that is all the scientist requires. In *Religion and Science* he brought this analysis to bear on the question of immortality. In discussions of immortality it is assumed that the personality of a dead person continues to exist, so he offered an analysis of 'personality' using as his base the ideas of *The Analysis of Mind*.

> Personality is essentially a matter of organization. Certain events, grouped together by means of certain relations, form a person. The grouping is effected by means of causal

laws – those connected with habit-formation, which includes memory – and the causal laws concerned depend upon the body. If this is true – and there are strong scientific grounds for thinking that it is – to expect a personality to survive the disintegration of the brain is like expecting a cricket club to survive when all its members are dead. (*1935*, 143.)

Life after death, then, is not even a possibility, but this did not faze him. 'I believe that when I die I shall rot, and nothing of my ego will survive' (*1957*, 43).

Russell has a reputation as an implacable foe of religion, and, as we have had occasion to see, much of his writing on religion fits that description. Organized religion – or the church – because its power was based upon fear, was the enemy of the values he wished to champion. Many churchmen reciprocated his feelings, and on occasion, in New York City in 1940 for instance, they were able to make him pay a price for his hostility. At other times, when he was mistakenly reported dead in China in 1921 for example, their feelings toward him found gentler expression. On that occasion a missionary newspaper noticed the event by printing: 'Missionaries may be pardoned for heaving a sigh of relief at the news of Mr Bertrand Russell's death' (*1968*, 132). While he was always critical of the church in his writings, he was not hostile to all of its teachings. The central place of love in Christian doctrine had great appeal for him and he frequently recommended it as a cure for international differences. Something of it too is to be found in his credo that 'the good life is one inspired by love and guided by knowledge' (*1957*, 44) which is central to his little book, *What I Believe*, first published in 1925.

Love is not the only teaching of Christianity worth preserving. Two others are worship and acquiescence. He reached this conclusion in 'The Essence of Religion', an essay written in 1912 near the high-water mark of his affair with Lady Ottoline Morrell and one for which he retained a lingering fondness. It begins by distinguishing a finite and an infinite part in the human mind: the finite part is partial and essentially concerned with self-preservation; the infinite part is impartial and, when dominant, 'leads to truth in thought, justice in action, and universal love in feeling' (*1961*, 566). The religious life is one in which the finite has surrendered dominance to the infinite part. Many find that this surrender is made easier by belief in a God who must be obeyed, but he denied that such a belief is essential to developing a religious outlook. Once the religious life is attained, the person will see that the Christian notions of worship, acquiescence and love are all desirable, if they can be freed of selectivity. Worship should be of two kinds: 'the one involving the goodness but not the existence of its object (the ideal); the other involving the existence but not the goodness of its object (what exists)'. Religious action will be the attempt to bridge the two, to make 'more good exist and more of existence good' (*1961*, 571). The Christian doctrine that we acquiesce in everything, he thought mistaken, because 'everything' includes what is evil. Rather, what is wanted is acquiescence in the inevitable without judging it to be good. We achieve the sort of acquiescence he recommended when we accept the inevitable, which we may think bad, without anger, indignation or regret. Finally, we should try to develop an impartial love towards all that exists; such love is both contemplative and active and is given without thought of benefiting its object. Religion, on this view, is an intensely individual matter; it suited its author, for Russell was never very comfortable in groups.

Russell often linked the religious outlook just described with mysticism; but most mystics made the mistake, or so he thought, of succumbing to the temptation to turn their insight into a set of beliefs. He thought that all such attempts are bound to fail, because only by the use of scientific method can what is true be established. Some mystical insights may, when tested, turn out to be true. But until they are tested it is a mistake to assume their truth. To resist the will to believe may be difficult, but he held that it is essential if one is to achieve a truly religious outlook.

IX
POLITICAL THEORY:
LIBERAL AND DEMOCRATIC

From the beginning to the end of his career Russell was interested in questions of political theory. He did not work at developing a position in this area with the same tenacity of purpose he displayed in logic and philosophy. Therefore, it is fair to say that he did not have the influence in politics that he had in the other two areas. Nevertheless many read him and found in his writings an important and persuasive defence of democracy against anti-democratic movements of both the left and the right.

His very first book, *German Social Democracy*, is a critical examination of Marxism in a German context. Shortly after their marriage, Russell and Alys spent several months in Berlin studying political economy. As a case study he focused upon the history of the social democratic movement in Germany. On the whole his book is sympathetic to this movement, but Marx himself he found both tedious (in *Capital*) and inspiring (in the *Communist Manifesto*, a work "almost unsurpassed in literary merit'). 'For terse eloquence, for biting wit, and for historical insight, it is, to my mind, one of the best pieces of political literature ever produced' (*1896*, 10) When, however, he came to examine the theory which Marx advanced to show the

95

inevitability of communism, he found little in it that is both true and important. Marx seemed to believe there is a connection between his materialism and his economics, which Russell summarized and criticized in this way: 'Since mind has been produced by matter, its ultimate motives for action are to be found in material things; the production of these is, accordingly, the moving force which underlies all human phenomena. This transition is nowhere clearly set forth, and is obviously incapable of logical proof' (*1896*, 7). The connection is, therefore, an article of faith, which led him to conclude that Marxism is really a new religion. This conclusion he found reinforced by the observation that Marx merely assumed the desirability of socialism. 'Marx professes to prove that Socialism *must* come', he wrote in *Roads to Freedom*, 'but scarcely concerns himself to argue that when it comes it will be a good thing. It may be, however, that if it comes, it will be a good thing, even though all Marx's arguments to prove that it must come should be at fault' (*1918*, 43). In later writings he was often to renew this charge that Marxism is a religion; in the chapter on St Augustine in his *History of Western Philosophy* he provided a dictionary by which the emotive words of the Judeo -Christian tradition are to be translated into the language of Marxism by the person who wants to understand Marx's psychology. The dogmatism of Marx and his followers was a chief reason for Russell's lifelong opposition to them.

Given the great importance of the thought of Marx for twentieth-century politics, it is appropriate, before turning to Russell's own political ideas, to discuss in more detail his critique of Marxism. Any writer on politics who hoped to secure an audience in the first half of the century, had to deal with Marx, who was everyone's rival, in some way. Russell, of course, tried to do it by showing that some central Marxian doctrines were faulty.

After Russell had abandoned Hegelianism, he viewed any use of the Hegelian dialectic with suspicion; he had seen the disaster it made of mathematics in the writings of Hegel himself. Since Marx used the Hegelian dialectic, Russell approached his work with the intention of examining the logic carefully. An amusing feature about the dialectic, to Russell's mind, was the claim by Hegel that it led to the Prussian state and the counterclaim by Marx that Prussia would be swept away by the dialectic. Another arresting feature of Marx's thought was its espousal of materialism. Hegel had coupled his method with an idealistic position in ontology: only minds and their contents were real. But for Marx only material objects were real, and mind was a mere property of their organization. Marx, then, from Russell's point of view, used a defective logic and he started from a metaphysical position, materialism, which might or might not embody truth. Russell did not think it was possible to know whether or not materialism is true. Marx's version of it might be true, but its truth cannot be known. Nor can the connection between materialism and economics be proved, as we have seen above. But, Russell argues, let us suppose that the connection holds. We still have to ask why change must be progressive. Socialism may be inevitable, but is it desirable? Death and taxes are inevitable too, but they are not always desirable. Inevitability and desirability are two quite separate matters. Marx professes to prove inevitability, but assumes desirability. If his proof of inevitability is wrong, socialism might still prove desirable. And even if it is inevitable, it might still prove to be bad. Russell thinks that Marx, along with many others of the time, simply accepted the prevailing doctrine of progress, and never seriously questioned it.

Turning to Marx's economics, Russell offers criticisms of both of his main doctrines: the theory of value, with its corollary, the theory of surplus value, and the law of the concentration of capital. As everyone knows, Marx held a version of the labour theory of value, in which the value of a commodity is measured by the labour that went into its production. Marx offers a proof that labour is the essence of value. It is possible, his argument begins, to equate the value of two different commodities. This is a measure of their exchange value, consequently their exchange value cannot uniquely belong to them, because it is equal for different things. What is it, then, that commodities have in common? According to Marx, only the property of having been produced by human labour – and what he calls 'undifferentiated human labour' at that; therefore, labour is the source of value, and quantity of value is measured by quantity of labour, which he took to be labour-time.

Russell brings two criticisms to bear on the form of this argument. (1) Marx claims by abstraction of differences to have hit upon the *only* property each commodity has in common with its fellows. This can go wrong in one of two ways. On the one hand, there may be other properties held in common by every commodity which have simply been overlooked. It is easy for us, when we have found one, to persuade ourselves that it is the only one. (2) There is no assurance that, even if we come up with one and only one common property, that it is relevant to the problem at hand. A separate argument must be advanced, for instance, to show that labour is related to value in the way claimed. Russell also criticizes the substance of Marx's purported proof. Marx claims that the only property all commodities share is their production by undifferentiated human labour. This is false, Russell argues, because it is clear that another common property of commodities is utility, or the power of satisfying a need. Utility, by Marx's own argument, has an good a claim to be called the essence of value as 'undifferentiated human labour' has.

Indeed, Russell thinks 'utility' has a much better claim, because it is capable of accounting for the fact that virgin land has a price. Marx could not deny that virgin land had a price, but he did claim that it had no value, because it is unmixed with human labour. So Marx concluded that the price was imaginary, on the analogy of imaginary numbers in mathematics. Russell presses his argument at this point. If virgin land has a price, even an imaginary one, then price must be the same as exchange-value, for it you sell the land to me in exchange for manufactured articles whose value is labour-determined, then by the equation of exchange-value you and I must agree that the virgin land in question has exchange-value; so virgin land has exchange-value after all, but presumably only in a normative sense. Is Marx, then, using 'value' in an ethical sense? Does he mean 'that goods *ought* to exchange in proportion to the labour involved, and would do so in a world ruled by economic justice' (1934, 235)? There is some independent evidence that Marx does sometimes use 'value' in an ethical sense, for he cites cases where value and price diverge as proof of the wickedness of capitalism. If this is true, then he has abandoned economics for ethics, and in place of analyzing economic facts he is setting up an economic ideal.

Such an economic ideal is impossible, Russell argues. Ricardo, in developing his theory of rent, considered the case of two bushels of wheat, one grown on bad land and one grown on good land. That grown on bad land embodies much more labour-time than that grown on good land, yet there is no imaginable economic system which would, on the same day, fix a higher price for the wheat grown on bad land. The advantage given the man with good land over that with marginal land is called 'rent' in economic theory. Russell does not think that Marx ever understood rent, essentially for the reasons already given: there was no place for it in his system. But it does seem to be an economic fact one cannot overlook, and one that is inextricably bound up with the value of commodities.

Let us turn now to Russell's critique of the theory of surplus value. Surplus value, according to Marx, is the value of a commodity above and beyond what was paid to the producer of it. Suppose a person to work eight hours for an entrepreneur and to produce two artifacts in that time. The entrepreneur pays the worker only a subsistence wage, which Marx estimated to be about half of the labour-time: in this hypothetical case, the value of one artifact. The other half, the 'surplus value', goes to the capitalist as his profit. 'Hence, by purchasing labour-power at the ordinary market rate, the capitalist is able to exploit the labourer, and grow rich by keeping the labourer at the starvation level' (*1896*, 17). This argument, Russell noted, is based upon two assumptions, neither of which is necessarily true. The first is that all labour has to be paid for. The necessity of making this assumption is seen when we reflect on the fact that, although the capitalist only pays for four hours work, he is able to price the artifact proportionally to the labour-time required for production, in this example, eight hours. Marx never gives any reason for supposing this true. The second assumption is that capitalists compete with one another to keep wages at a subsistence level. At best, Russell thinks, this is only sometimes true, since combinations and cartels are frequently met with in the history of capitalism. Russell thought that Marx did not give proper credit to the efforts of the capitalist, who supplies a great deal of value to his enterprise, yet because of his theory of value, Marx is unable to take this factor into account. Marx's viewpoint, Russell suggests, prohibits him from being subtle enough in his economic analysis. From the worker's point of view what is not wages is non-wages; the worker does not distinguish within non-wages, profit from rent and capital, but the economist must. By deliberately adopting the worker's stance, Marx to that extent abandoned the economist's.

With respect to Marx's second important economic doctrine, the law of the concentration of capital, we can be briefer. Marx held that with the passage of time capital becomes concentrated in fewer and fewer hands within a given industry, until each industry is monopolized. This happens because competition forces weak sisters to the wall where they either perish or are merged into their competition. While recognizing an element of truth in this for certain industries in certain countries, Russell thinks that on the whole it is false. Most companies are stock-companies and so tend to have many stockholders, all of whom are Marxian capitalists. The existence of large numbers of stock-holders seems to contradict Marx's law; and agriculture does not come under it at all. It is true that there are very large land-holders, but a land-holder is not a farmer, and only farming is capitalistic. Russell thinks that Marx confuses landlords and farmers.

A further deficiency of Marx's economics, to Russell's mind, is its failure to take demand into account. It is fairly easy to think of examples where the amount of labour-time in two commodities is the same, but the one sells like hot-cakes and the other gathers dust on the shelf. Demand must find a place in any adequate economic theory.

It is obvious that Russell finds Marxism wanting. In his youth Russell was attracted to Marx and hoped to find in his writings doctrines with which he could agree, but the more he read him the more disillusioned he became. The metaphysical base was a liability and the economic theory seriously deficient. These alone would be reason enough to reject Marxism, but, when Russell came to think very seriously about political questions during the First World War, he became aware of another serious shortcoming in Marx's political theory, and that was its underlying psychology. 'The material-istic theory of history, in the last analysis, requires the assumption that every politically conscious person is governed by one single desire – the desire to increase his own share of commodities; and further, that his method of achieving this desire will usually be to seek to increase the share of his class, not only his own individual share' (*1920*, 80). Russell agrees with Marx that all politics is governed by human desires, but he thinks the list of desires is longer than that presented by

Marx, for instance, the desire for power is an obvious motive not included by Marx. To gain power some people will readily pass up the chance to make fortunes; such people within a state, and especially within a communistic state, are likely to prove disruptive. A more generous psychology than that allowed by Marx is required for an understanding of politics; Russell's own political theory will seek to remedy this deficiency.

After *German Social Democracy* Russell did not have occasion to write again on questions of political theory until he found himself engulfed in the First World War. That such madness had come to pass showed the failure of the prevailing philosophy of politics. If future wars were to be rendered impossible, some political reconstruction would be required after the war was over. His theory was published as *Principles of Social Reconstruction* in 1916; the American edition was renamed *Why Men Fight* by the publisher without consulting him, presumably on the ground that its sales would be greater. His basic point in this work is that war, and aggressive behaviour generally, can be traced to the thwarting of the principle of growth which is present in each of us and which is on the whole benign. This principle is the source of our impulses and desires, some of which have to be checked if we are to live in harmony with one another. If they are checked in brutal and unreasoning ways, then the energy required to restrain them out of fear of punishment is likely also to nourish certain destructive impulses and desires, such as the desire for revenge. He believed, and here education assumes a key role in his theory and a growing one in his interests, that the impulses and desires requiring discouragement should, in the first instance, be allowed to dissipate. When they are gone, the child should be taken in hand by a teacher and given reasons for restraining such impulses and desires should they arise again. Bottling them up will lead to explosions and, when whole populations are similarly affected, even to wars.

The burden of the book is to argue for a democratic state in which the citizenry has been educated to develop its creative impulses and desires and to control its destructive ones. Control will come, he argued, if children are taught to think. The prevailing educational system takes children who enjoy thinking and teaches them to stop thinking. His reflections on this dreary state of affairs led him to write one of his best known and most arresting passages.

> Men fear thought as they fear nothing else on earth – more than ruin, more even than death. Thought is subversive and revolutionary, destructive and terrible; thought is merciless to privilege, established institutions, and comfortable habits; thought is anarchic and lawless, indifferent to authority, careless of the well-tried wisdom of the ages. Thought looks into the pit of hell and is not afraid. It sees man, a feeble speck, surrounded by unfathomable depths of silence; yet it bears itself proudly, as unmoved as if it were lord of the universe. Thought is great and swift and free, the light of the world, and the chief glory of man. (*1916*, 165–6.)

In *The ABC of Relativity* (1925) he remarked again on the way in which the prevailing educational system turns out adults who are afraid of thought, and the terrible consequence some of them suffer: 'We all have a tendency to think that the world must conform to our prejudices. The opposite view involves some effort of thought, and most people would die sooner than think – in fact, they do so' (166).

His rethinking of the foundations of politics led him to reject State socialism as the best solution for the problems of the working class. Socialism, whether Marxist or not, has too narrow a view of the problems of the working man, putting too much emphasis upon income, and tacitly assuming that if income is improved the recipient of it will be made happy. He did not think this was likely to prove true. Replacing the capitalist by the State still leaves the worker alienated from the process of which he is an essential part. What is required for happiness is that the worker's creative impulses be essentially involved in the whole process of production. From this premiss he argued for some form of workers' control of industry. The State, to his mind, should remain aside to function as a arbitrator when industrial democracy fails to settle a given question, and experience has shown that an arbitrator will often be needed.

Political Ideals (1917), delivered as a set of lectures while the First World War was in progress and published at the time only in the United States, uses the ideas developed in *Principles of Social Reconstruction*. Impulses are distinguished into those that are creative and those that are possessive, permitting him to give an account of power or force as something essentially linked to possessive impulses. 'Material possessions can be taken by force and enjoyed by the robber. Spiritual possessions cannot be taken in this way' (*1917*, 9). It is hardly surprising to learn therefore that 'the best life is the one in which the creative impulses play the largest part and the possessive impulses the smallest' (8). The argument of the book favours liberal democracy: 'It is not one ideal for all men, but a separate ideal for each separate man, that has to be realized if possible' (5–6).

In 1918 when he published *Roads to Freedom* he took up the question of which of three competing theories – socialism, anarchism and syndicalism – promise the best answers to the problem of reconstruction with the least bureaucracy. Of the three he thought syndicalism holds the greatest promise and socialism the least. Anarchism, towards which he showed a degree of sympathy which later (when he wrote a new Preface in 1949) he thought unjustified, holds a middle position. Syndicalism 'is concerned with reforming actual work and the organization of industry, not *merely* with securing greater rewards for work' (*1918a*, 75). In attempting to achieve their ends syndicalists favour industrial over political action. Industrial action includes strikes, especially the General Strike, boycotts and sabotage. Its theorists believe that if they can bring about the General Strike they will bring down the State, thus emancipating the workers, because they see the State as the guarantor of the capitalist. Pure syndicalism, in his opinion, goes too far in the direction of radical change. For Britain, guild socialism, which owes much to syndicalism, holds the greatest promise. Guild socialists aim at curtailing the power of the State by gaining autonomy for industry. An organization parallel to the existing political structure would be set up, if guild socialists had their way, topped by a Guild Congress co-equal to Parliament. Together they would govern the country: Parliament would concern itself with the interests of the consumers, the Guild Congress with the interests of the producers. The practical details of how such a system could be made to work are given neither by the guild socialists not by Russell. It is not at all apparent how disputes between the Guild Congress and Parliament would be resolved; one or other of them must have the final word, but that would seem to vitiate the theory of the guild socialists.

The Practice and Theory of Bolshevism came out in 1920. It was written after a journey to the new Soviet Union to see at first hand what the Bolsheviks were up to in their new state. In 1917 he had gone to Leeds to join with others on the left in celebrating the overthrow of the Tsar. He went to Russia prepared to approve of what he saw, but he came back profoundly disappointed and his book registers that disappointment. Rather surprisingly, given his earlier political writings, he stated that he believed that 'communism is necessary to the world' (*1920*, 6) but Bolshevism is not. Part of his critique charged Bolshevism with an inadequate psychology. The analysis of human motivation first stated in *Principles of Social Reconstruction* was expanded and refined: people are moved by desires for food, drink, sex and shelter; these he called primitive desires. When satisfaction of them is threatened, almost any reaction is possible. In addition to the primitive desires, and often closely associated with them, are four secondary desires or passions which, along with the primitive ones, account for nearly all political activity. The four are acquisitiveness, vanity, rivalry, and love of power. The Bolsheviks make the mistake of omitting the last three from their repertoire. He predicted that love of power, abetted by vanity, will gradually bring about a vast centralized bureaucracy which would, in practice, re-establish class divisions. A more sophisticated state structure based upon a better psychology would avoid this unwelcome prospect, but the Bolsheviks are trapped by their own dogma. Following Marx, they have made of their theories a religion. His friends on the left were dismayed with the very negative position that Russell took towards Bolshevism. He did not, however, have to regret what he said: in 1949 in a new Preface to the book he said that it had proved unnecessary to revise it because events had confirmed the hypotheses he had advanced in it. About the only changes he made for the new edition was the occasional replacement of 'communism' by 'socialism'.

Foundational questions of politics did not engage his attention again until 1938 when he published *Power*. By this time he had concluded that 'love of power is the chief motive producing the changes which social science has to study' (*1938*, 13). Love of power is an infinite desire, as is love of glory, by which he meant that they have no limit of satisfaction. Power, like energy, takes many forms, none of which are subordinate to the others. The various manifestations of power, e.g. wealth and armaments, have a way of changing into one another, so they cannot be studied in isolation from one another without introducing serious error. Social scientists should attempt to discover the laws which govern the transformations of power; as a suggestion for where they should begin, he offered extended analyses of each kind of power and suggested some preliminary hypotheses regarding transformations, which, may, when refined and tested, prove to be true. And as one expects he would do, he suggested ways in which power might be tamed.

After the Second World War he concerned himself with two large questions of politics: the proper relationship between governmental authority and the individual and the effects of science on political and social life. His answer to the first, given in *Authority and the Individual* (1949), makes use of the conceptual framework of his First World War books. The problem is to find a way for our impulses, especially the creative ones, to have an area for their expression in a world where authority has been on the increase. The answer, he thought, was to be found in decentralized authority. There should be a world government, now that there are atomic bombs, but its authority should be limited to matters of war and peace. The other areas of life where some authority is required should be regulated at the lowest level of government compatible with maintaining public order. The tendency has been for governments to centralize authority, taking up to higher levels what was formerly done at lower levels. They have not done things better, so it is time to reverse the process and decentralize authority again.

The question of world peace became more urgent after the explosion of the first Russian A-bomb, so *New Hopes for a Changing World* (1951) urged again the necessity of instituting a world government. World government offers the only way of taming the genie that science has released from its bottle. If that genie can be tamed, then scientific efforts can be diverted to making human life much happier than it has ever been before. His book concludes with his vision of the happy world. In this world an international government would control the production and distribution of food and raw materials, enforce universal birth-control, and have a monopoly on armed force; but the constitution of such a world government must ensure rights for every person and must provide educational institutions which will encourage and develop the innate capacities of individuals to their highest perfection. Such a world would be 'not only happy but glorious':

I cannot believe that what is dark and dreadful and destructive in the souls of men is essential to the production of great works of imagination. I believe, on the contrary, that it lies within the power of man to create edifices of shining splendor, from which the glory and greatness of which human thought and feeling are capable shall spread a light unmixed with darkness, filling men's hearts with joy and their thoughts with clarity. Such a world is possible. It rests with men to choose whether they will create it, or allow the human race to perish in anger and sordid hate. (*1951a*, 217; *1951b*, 212)

In *The Impact of Science on Society* (1952) he examined once again the way in which the rise of science has altered human society; he had first done it in *The Scientific Outlook* in 1931 where he painted a chilling picture of a society in which science had run amok. When Aldous Huxley published *Brave New World* in 1932 Russell wrote to his publisher suggesting that the plot of that book had been taken from *The Scientific Outlook* and wondering what, if anything, he should do about it. Unwin discouraged any action. In *Impact of Science on Society* he is concerned to bring the topic up to date. In addition to its effects on our intellects – it has rid us of many traditional but unsupported beliefs – science has led to the rise of industry, with all its benefits, as well as revolutionized warfare, with all its horrors. Its latest product, the H-bomb, has made world government necessary, but it will probably, he feared, take another war to achieve it. In his conclusion he listed the conditions necessary for the stability of the new scientific society in which we find ourselves. The list is a daunting one: world government, a redistribution of wealth among nations, a static population, ample opportunity for personal initiative, and the greatest possible diffusion of power. The world is far from realizing these conditions, so 'we must expect vast upheavals and appalling suffering before stability is attained' (*1952*, 139–40). In spite of this gloomy prognosis, he still thought one should cling to the hope that has been glimpsed, that science one day will be a force only for good.

Except for some essays on civil disobedience, the last work in which he discussed political theory is *Human Society in Ethics and Politics*. The most theoretical chapter on politics is 'Politically Important Desires', his Nobel Prize acceptance speech. 'All human activity is prompted by desire or impulse' (160) establishes at once that his position has not changed since 1916; and when he lists the desires that move people as 'acquisitiveness, rivalry, vanity, and love of power' (161), all of which he claims are infinite in the sense that they can never be fully satisfied, we find that he had not altered the refinements he made to his theory in the years between the two wars. The political half of the book is basically a recapitulation of his thinking of the preceding forty years.

One feature of his political writings underscores just how much of a Victorian he remained. Very often we find him expressing with great passion the view that, if only human beings would listen to him and act on what he recommends, then they would, collectively, progress until paradise is reached. And he does not shrink from using the words 'paradise' and 'utopia'. But in other writings, when he is discussing the Victorian era, he slates it for its uncritical belief in progress. The outbreak of the First World War put an end to such nonsense, he tells us sternly. Bergson and Spencer are raked over the coals for constructing philosophies based upon evolution and its implicit idea of progress. 'A process which led from the amoeba to Man appeared to the philosophers to be obviously a progress – though whether the amoeba would agree with this opinion is not known' (*1918*, 24). In their writings, evolutionists deceive their readers into accepting mere change as progress: 'Somehow, without explicit statement, the assurance is slipped in that the future, though we cannot foresee it, will be better than the past or the present: the reader is like the child which expects a sweet because it has been told to open its mouth and shut its eyes' (*ibid.*). It is true, of course, that the philosophers he criticized viewed progress as a natural and inevitable process, whereas he speaks of it as normative. They told people that circumstances would continue to improve until some ideal state was reached; he told people what they ought to do in order to achieve utopia. But the passion with which he expressed his belief in the perfectibility of human kind, as in the quotation from *New Hopes for a Changing World* above, seems effectively to reduce the distance between him and the evolutionists. Given his great care to express himself carefully in his purely philosophical writings, one would expect that he would have been content to draw the conclusion, in his political arguments, that the world would be a better place, to some measurable degree, if his advice was followed; but instead we frequently find him writing in superlatives, and extreme superlatives at that. What we must notice, in order to make some sense of this, is that he did not regard his political writings as in any way philosophical. In discussing his method he wrote: 'A philosopher is expected to tell us something about the nature of the universe as a whole, and to give grounds

for either optimism or pessimism. Both these expectations seem to me mistaken' (*1918*, 98). But that leaves
it open to him to opt for either a pessimistic or an
optimistic outlook, and to support his choice with
persuasive arguments. Throughout his life, even when
he most despaired of his fellow human beings, it was a
resurgence of the optimism of his youth which restored
his balance.

Surveying his writings on political theory one
conclusion emerges pretty plainly: he was throughout
his life a defender of liberal democracy. It is true that
he did flirt with other political theories from time to
time, but upon examination these flirtations appear of
limited extent; he was usually casting about for ideas to
remedy some deficiency in the liberal democratic state.
He was a staunch defender of individual rights,
including the right to participate in government, and
such rights are denied in whole or in part by a number
of the political theories which have had a vogue in the
twentieth century. Only the democracies have consis-
tently tried, and then not always successfully, to
guarantee the political rights of their citizens. From
his writings it is plain that Russell always assumed that
those in governmental positions have a duty to respect
the rights of those they govern, however disagreeable
they find those people to be who are exercising their
right to speak or assemble or protest. His own actions
often tried, and occasionally broke, the patience of
government officials, but he seems never to have feared
that they would not respect his right to make his case.
He assumed that they agreed with him that liberal
democracy, with all its imperfections and trials, was
worth preserving.

X
POLITICAL ACTIVISM:
HIS DUTY TO HIS FAMILY

From earliest childhood he had been taught, principally by his grandmother, that political activism was the duty of a Russell. On the flyleaf of a Bible she gave him as a birthday present, she wrote one of her favourite verses: 'Thou shalt not follow a multitude to do evil.' 'Her emphasis upon this text', Russell noted many years later, 'led me in later life to be not afraid of belonging to small minorities' (*1967*, 22; *1967a*, 18). It was expected of him that he would channel his activism into a political career, as his grandfather had done so successfully and his father had tried but failed to do, thus ensuring that the family tradition was carried on. After his grandfather's death his grandmother continued to interest herself in political matters; she was especially passionate about the prospects for Italian unity and a settlement of the Irish question. In discussing these and other political issues with Bertrand she impressed upon him the importance of preparing himself to help resolve such problems when he grew up. The lessons obviously took. 'My family during four centuries was important in the political life of England, and I was brought up to feel a responsibility which demanded that I should express my opinion on political questions. This feeling is more deeply implanted in me than reason would warrant' (*1956a*, 48).

115

During his young manhood political activities took a definite second place to his intellectual work. He did find time to agitate, mostly by writing, for free trade, and, partly because of Alys's influence, for woman's suffrage. His pamphlet, *Anti-Suffragist Anxieties* (1910) is an acute analysis of the arguments which were being advanced against votes for women; he found all of them logically deficient and he thought all of them manufactured as a cover for the real reason some men opposed the enfranchisement of women:

> The objections which are explicitly urged against women's suffrage are, of course, not those which weigh most with most men. Men fear that their liberty to act in ways that are injurious to women will be curtailed, and that they will lose that pleasing sense of dominion what at present makes 'no place like home'. The instinct of the master to retain his mastery cannot be met by mere political arguments. But it is an instinct which finds less and less scope in the modern world, and it is fast being driven from this stronghold as it has been driven from others. To substitute cooperation for subjection is everywhere the effort of democracy, and it is one of the strongest arguments in favour of the enfranchisement of women that it will further this substitution in all that concerns the relations of men and women. (*1985*, 315–6.)

In 1907 he was nominated by the National Union of Suffrage Societies to contest a Parliamentary by-election in Wimbledon. At the time he was a member of the Liberal Party, and, except for the issue of women's suffrage which his own party opposed, he based his campaign on Liberal positions; as expected, he lost the election by a wide margin and returned to work on *Principia Mathematica*.

The outbreak of war in August 1914 transformed him from a logician with an interest in social and political questions into a political activist who used his great command of logic to demolish the positions of his opponents. For a number of years he had claimed to be a pacifist of sorts, ever since the famous conversion experience brought about by witnessing Evelyn Whitehead's suffering, but there had been no occasion for testing his belief. When war broke out he found himself overwhelmed by anti-war feelings and immediately concluded that anti-war work must have top priority in his life. To his utter dismay he found that many, who before the war had agreed theoretically with him on pacifism, were just as strongly swept away by pro-war feelings. Some old friends and associates stood firm, however, and they offered him an emotional base from which to work.

It must be stressed that his position was opposition to the war then in progress, what we, in retrospect, call the First World War. He was not, then or ever, opposed to all wars; he was not, then or ever, a complete pacifist in the way some Quakers are. To make his position clear he wrote an essay, 'The Ethics of War', which is reprinted in *Justice in War-Time* (1916), in which he considers whether any war can be justified and argues that some can be. Justified wars fall into three classes: (a) some past wars of colonization in which the more civilized drove the less civilized from their land, thus spreading civilization, which he judges to be good; (b) some past (and likely future) wars of principle, such as the American Civil War which abolished slavery and therefore aided progress; (c) some past (and very likely future) wars of self-defence, even though it is often difficult to determine whether a given war is a pure specimen of this sort or one of a different kind dressed up as a war of self-defence. Only wars of prestige are always to be condemned, for there are other, and better, ways to settle the differences involved. The war then being fought was, in its origins, a war of prestige, and, as such, earned his condemnation. Publishing his belief that some wars are justified made close work with Quakers and other complete pacifists a delicate matter; they would have preferred that his great passion not have such a narrow target.

Anti-war agitation brought him twice to court to defend himself against charges of violating war-time legislation. The facts regarding his first case have been laid out in the first chapter. His conviction did not slow his opposition to the war; he continued for another eighteen months to pour nearly all of his energy into it. Late in 1917 he let it be known that with the coming of the new year he would be dropping out of pacifist work and resuming philosophical research. A point was made of informing the Government of his intentions; his brother, then a Labour peer, personally visited the appropriate Ministers to inform them. Having concluded that his opposition to the war, whose end now seemed in sight as the United States became more involved, had been fruitless, and that he could give the world much more of more certain value if he resumed what he was unquestionably good at, namely philosophy, he felt a certain relief. But he could not abandon his anti-war associates too abruptly, and when, very early in 1918, they required a front-page article for *The Tribunal* and turned to him, he obliged them. 'The German Peace Offer', published on 3 January, contained a sentence which the Government claimed insulted an ally: 'The American Garrison which will by that time be occupying England and France, whether or not they will prove efficient against the

Germans, will no doubt be capable of intimidating strikers, an occupation to which the American Army is accustomed when at home.' (It has always seemed to me that it is the next two sentences whose publication galled the authorities, but about which they could manufacture no case: 'I do not say that these thoughts are in the mind of the Government. All the evidence tends to show that there are no thoughts whatever in their mind, and that they live from hand to mouth consoling themselves with ignorance and sentimental twaddle.') Russell was charged under the Defence of the Realm Act with having published a statement likely to prejudice the British Government's relations with the United States; he was tried, found guilty, and sentenced to six months in prison. On appeal his prison sentence was altered from Second to First Division. In the First Division he had to pay rent for his cell but he could have his own furniture; he could pay another prisoner to keep his cell clean; he could also have books and writings materials; and he could have more visitors and more letters than Second Division prisoners were allowed. During his imprisonment he wrote one of his best books, *Introduction to Mathematical Philosophy* (1919), a more popular account of the argument of *Principia Mathematica*.

The causes in which he was active in the period between the two world wars were in general those taken up by the non-communist left, such as reform in education, dissemination of information about birth-control, reform of the divorce laws, independence for India, and world peace. As Hitler rose, so did Russell's fears of another world war. In 1936 he published *Which Way to Peace?*, a topical book concerned to discuss the policy which Great Britain should adopt given the destructive power of aerial bombing and the increasing likelihood of war due to Hitler's policies. A number of alternatives – isolationism, collective security agreements, and alliances – are examined and found wanting. Casting about for a policy, he took up the case for complete pacifism, or unilateral disarmament, and, arguing by analogy from the case of Denmark, he concluded that Britain would be better off under this policy than under any of its alternatives. The adoption of such a policy requires that the population free itself of fear, pride and greed. Since these feelings are widespread, it is very unlikely that by use of argument alone the whole population can be freed of them. He is not, therefore, very hopeful that war can be avoided, but he assures the reader that he is recommending the policy of complete pacifism only for Britain and only for the present time; his reason is that air warfare has become so destructive that desperate measures are necessary to meet the threat of it. He has not himself adopted complete pacifism:

> I am not a believer in the doctrine of non-resistance; I do not desire the abolition of the police; I do not hold that war is always and everywhere a crime. ... I am not prepared always to condemn *civil* wars; the Spanish Government is obviously right to resist its rebels. (*1936*, 151–2.)

Anyone who adopts pacifism as his or her policy, he warns, must avoid becoming fanatical about it, for a fanatical pacifist is an ineffective pacifist. For the foreseeable future it is extremely unlikely that pacifists will assume the government of Britain, so individual pacifists are going to have to find within themselves the resources to act alone or with a handful of others when war comes. Here of course his counsel was based upon his own searing experiences during the First World

War. Throughout the book there is the assumption that
Russell himself would remain a pacifist during the
coming conflict, but when war did come he gradually
found his opposition to it being eroded. On 11
February 1941 he wrote a long letter to *The New York
Times* explaining that he was not opposed to the war
then engulfing Europe. His reason is of a piece with the
position he had always defended; this was a war of
principle and he approved of the principle: 'There came
a moment – some will say one moment, some another –
when it became evident that Germany would destroy
the independence of the democracies one by one if they
did not combine in armed defence. From that moment
the only hope for democracy was war.'

After returning to England in the summer of 1944 he
spent the next decade as the nearest thing to an estab-
lishment politician as he was ever to be. Shortly after
the war was over, he addressed the House of Lords on
the dangers of the atomic bomb. As early as 1923, in
The ABC of Atoms, he had warned that the new
physics might lead to such a weapon: 'It is remarkable
that, like Einstein's theory of gravitation, a great deal of
the work on the structure of the atom was done during
the war. It is probable that it will ultimately be used for
making more deadly explosives and projectiles than any
yet invented' (*1923*, 11). In the late 1940s he lectured
to Generals in War Colleges, outlining for them his
view of the international situation, a prominent aspect
of which was the threat posed by the Soviet Union for
the Western democracies. For a brief inglorious period
he even advocated that the United States threaten the
Union of Soviet Socialist Republics with pre-emptive
war to prevent it acquiring nuclear weaponry.

After Russia exploded its first atom bomb and the
United States its first hydrogen bomb, his alarm at the

bleak outlook for human life mounted; he felt he had to do something to try to lower the risk of nuclear war. As he was accustomed to do in such times of crisis, he turned to the power of his pen. At Christmastime in 1954 he read over the BBC his famous essay, 'Man's Peril from the Hydrogen Bomb'. 'Here, then, is the problem I present to you, stark and dreadful and inescapable: Shall we put an end to the human race; or shall mankind renounce war?' (*1956a*, 217). The black consequences of the first alternative are laid out in order to increase the attractiveness of the second. He appeals to the neutral nations to combine so as to form a morally powerful group which may, in time, mediate the differences between the two great powers; and he appeals to everyone capable of rational thought to do their bit towards making war obsolete. The tide might be turned by political activity on the part of those heretofore unpolitical. The concluding paragraph is full of passion:

> I cannot believe that this is to be the end. I would have men forget their quarrels for a moment and reflect that, if they will allow themselves to survive, there is every reason to expect the triumphs of the future to exceed immeasurably the triumphs of the past. There lies before us, if we choose, continual progress in happiness, knowledge, and wisdom. Shall we, instead, choose death because we cannot forget our quarrels? I appeal, as a human being to human beings: remember your humanity, and forget the rest. If you can do so, the way lies open to a new Paradise; if you cannot, nothing lies before you but universal death. (*1956a*, 220.)

Public response to his broadcast was very strong. Something had to be done to channel this energy into organized activities which just might turn the tide in favour of peace. His first move, suggested by his receipt of a letter from Frédéric Joliot-Curie, an eminent French physicist who was also a member of the Communist Party, was to prepare a manifesto, to be signed only by leading scientists from both the East and the West, calling for a meeting of scientists whose task it would be to persuade their governments to modify their policies. Russell drafted the manifesto and Einstein signed it a few days before he died. The first meeting of scientists, at Pugwash in Nova Scotia, the summer home of Cyrus Eaton who funded it, was held in 1957. The Pugwash Conferences, as they have come to be called, continued throughout the Cold War; their participants seem agreed that the contacts established at these conference helped reduce the level of tension felt between East and West. Russell had an interview with Nehru, then the Prime Minister of India, and tried to persuade him to organize the neutral nations into a bloc. Success here was slower and less conclusively established, but gradually there came to be meetings of the neutrals, although their agendas did not include the sort of political activism that Russell had urged they undertake.

Since the leadership of the neutrals was uncertain, he and others were attracted by the thought that if Great Britain were divested of nuclear weapons then she could assume the leadership of the neutrals. It was a goal worth working for, and it fitted Britain's historical role; she had often stood aside while two groups of European nations attempted to achieve a balance of power between them and had become involved only when the balance began to shift too markedly in one direction. Russell's attraction to the idea was not new, for he had advocated it in *Which Way to Peace?* Many others now favoured the idea, so the Campaign for Nuclear Disarmament (CND) was born early in 1958, with Russell as President and Canon L. John Collins as Chairman. Once again, as he had in the First World War, Russell, who was militantly anti-religious, joined forces with religious people to fight the good fight. CND was remarkably successful as a mass organization. By the autumn of 1960 it appeared as if it might persuade a majority of the Labour Party Conference to adopt a policy of nuclear disarmament for Britain. Indeed Labour did vote in favour of the policy at its meeting in Scarborough, but a later conference reversed it. Scarborough proved the high-water mark for CND.

CND relied upon persuasion and peaceful demonstrations to gain its ends. Despite its success, Russell came to believe that the means which CND favoured were not sufficient to win its end. More direct action was required, in particular, civil disobedience. A proposal that members of CND deliberately break the law split the organization in two. The Committee of 100, which followed Russell, adopted civil disobedience as a means it would sometimes use. His argument was this: if enough people were willing to engage in acts of civil disobedience, the Government would give in to their demands rather than face the colossal task of dealing with such a multitude of law-breakers. The will of the Government had to be tested, so a demonstration was called. It went off as planned, and no one was arrested, so another demonstration was called for Hiroshima Day, 6 August 1961, during which Russell was stopped by the police from speaking in Hyde Park, London. The rest of the demonstration went off without a hitch, but a month later both Russell and his wife, along with other leaders of The Committee of 100, were ordered to appear in court where they were charged with inciting the population to commit acts of civil disobedience. After trial and conviction the Russells were sentenced to two months imprisonment, which, on appeal, was reduced to one week in the prison hospital. This series of actions, which received wide publicity, did more for his cause, in the short run at least, than almost any other move the authorities might have made.

In the long run, however, the authorities did have their way. By selecting, at demonstrations, those who were the organizers and administrators of The Committee of 100, for arrest, prosecution and imprisonment, they effectively crippled the organization. It never became the force that CND had been in its heyday. Russell himself must bear some responsibility for its decline; he became progressively more extreme in his published statements, thereby alienating many who had been his supporters; and he also became, what he had never been in his long life, anti-American. The Vietnam War fixed his anti-Americanism. Some of his most extreme statements, in a lifetime of extreme statements, were made with regard to it; and he matched words with deeds, sponsoring The International War Crimes Tribunal to try President Johnson and others *in absentia* for war crimes committed in Vietnam. The collection of papers he wrote about the war, *War Crimes in Vietnam* (1967), is perhaps his most passionate book.

During October and November of 1962 Russell involved himself in two international disputes about which he later wrote a book, *Unarmed Victory* (1963). The first was the Cuban missile crisis. From surveillance photographs the United States learned that the Soviet Union was installing missiles in Cuba. The installation was incomplete but Soviet ships were on their way to Cuba with more equipment and missiles. President Kennedy ordered a naval embargo of Cuba, which brought the dispute to flashpoint. Russell wrote letters and sent telegrams to the principal parties, pleading for a peaceful resolution. Both Kennedy and Premier Khrushchev replied, with messages clearly intended for the other side. After a scary few days, the Soviet Union backed down and ordered its ships, which were still in international waters, to return home. The other dispute was one regarding the border between China and India. Again his involvement consisted of pleas to the parties to settle it peacefully, and again his letters and telegrams were answered. In effect, as in the Cuban crisis, he offered himself as an intermediary, by which messages could be passed that both sides wanted the other side's public to know. This crisis lost much of its steam when the Chinese government declared a ceasefire and withdrew its troops to a line which satisfied the Indians. In such complex matters it is nearly impossible to judge, with any accuracy, whether or not Russell's intervention had any effect on the outcome. In such large international disputes it seems unlikely that the intervention of any outsider, however eminent, makes a crucial difference, unless, of course, one or other of the powers concerned decides to make use of the intervention for their own ends. No doubt Russell took this into his calculations; but the cause of world peace was so urgent that he would not have minded putting himself in a position where he risked being used on its behalf.

Even such a brief account of his political activism as this one makes two observations possible. The first of these concerns the role of history in his activism. All his life he was conscious, thanks to the success of his grandmother's teaching, of feeling historically important simply because he was a Russell. Part of what both she and he understood by this was that his actions should be informed by family history. The Russells had, by the stands they had taken over the centuries, established a family reputation of being on the reforming side of public issues. Awareness that one is on the reforming side requires knowledge of the past, so the study of history occupies a central place in the education of a Russell. The second observation concerns the role of education itself. By definition a reformer is one who attempts to change the opinions and attitudes of those who actions he or she would alter; new ways of thinking have to be established. His experience during the First World War led Russell to conclude that the education of most adults left them incapable of entertaining new hypotheses. Since they lacked this fundamental capacity, the reformer could not hope to change them. The sort of reform Russell wanted, therefore, would have to start with the educational system and try to alter it in such a way as to turn out people who were, to the limits of their natural abilities, able to think for themselves. Until people were able to think for themselves, agitation for reform was unlikely to succeed in bringing about change.

XI
THE IMPORTANCE OF THE STUDY OF HISTORY

As a child Russell developed a love for the reading of history which was a great joy to him throughout his life. But it was not only the pleasure he derived from it, great as that was, that led him to write essays urging others to adopt his habit of reading history books, it was also because he was persuaded, and again he cited his own experience as evidence, that people who knew some history are better able to cope with life's problems. In addition to these essays he also tried his hand at writing history. *The Problem of China* (1922) is, for the most part, a political history of that country; *Freedom and Organization* (1934) is his account of the political history of Europe and the United States from 1814 to 1914; and *A History of Western Philosophy* (1945) is a highly individualistic treatment of some of the great philosophers (and a few lesser ones) and their writings about which he thought he had something fresh to say. In that book he doubly emphasized its historical character by discussing also the political and social circumstances in which the philosopher under discussion worked.

'Of all the studies by which men acquire citizenship of the intellectual commonwealth, no single one is so indispensable as the study of the past' (*1961, 521*).

With this ringing sentence he opens his first essay on the value of historical study. 'On History' was published in 1904 and is, in part, intended as an answer to a new school of historians then making themselves heard. They claimed that the value of history derives from its truth and that it has no value beyond its truth; Russell agreed with the first part of their position, but not with the second part. History has value, in addition to its truth, because it enlarges the imagination and suggests actions and feelings that may otherwise never fall within the reader's experience. The person who knows some history will be a richer and, in his opinion, better person than one who is ignorant of the past. We come to terms with the past by studying it; that is the only means we have of mastering it. If we fail to master the past, it will master us.

To prepare the way for his own conception of the value of history, he must show that the conception of the new school of historians is deficient. His main criticism is that they have not thought their own position through. Their stance makes historical documents all important; the historian should ensure that no element of interpretation enters into his work on them. 'Objectivity before all things is to be sought, they tell us; let the facts be merely narrated and allowed to speak for themselves – if they can find tongues. It follows, as a part of the position, that all facts are equally important' (*1961*, *521*). In practice, however, the historian finds that he has to select among the facts; this all historians admit, but they do not often realize an important consequence of their admission. To select among facts, all of which are true, requires some criterion of value other than truth; therefore, truth cannot be the whole of history's value.

What principle of selection is to be used? One candidate is the scientific one: those facts are selected which support general laws. Introduction of this principle of selection assumes that history is at present a science, which is far from being the case. It may one day become a science, but even that may be doubted. The reason for the doubt is that in science generalizations based upon facts are accorded a higher value than the individual facts themselves, but this is not true of history; and it is difficult to see that it would become true if well-supported generalizations were discovered. To him it seems very likely that some historical facts will be highly valued in themselves however developed a science history becomes. If history's sole value is its truth, the value of individual facts would diminish as the system of scientific generalizations grew. He concludes that history has value other than its truth: namely, its utility in enlarging the imagination.

In this early essay there is not as much emphasis on the sheer pleasure to be derived from the reading of well-written history as there is in his other statements of history's case. In *How to Read and Understand History: The Past as the Key to the Future*, a Big Blue Book written in 1943 for that extraordinary American publisher, E. Haldeman-Julius, he restated his case for the importance of history but with greater stress upon the pleasure to be derived from its study. 'My subject is history as a pleasure, as an agreeable and profitable way of spending such leisure as an exacting world may permit. I am not a professional historian, but I have read much history as an amateur. My purpose is to try to say what I have derived from history, and what many others, I am convinced, could derive without aiming at becoming specialists' (*1957a*, 9). The pleasure, to be sure, will be immediate, although some of it will linger in memory. Every child should be taught some history, and efforts should be made to make it as interesting as a respect for the facts will allow; but even when this has been done it will not be everyone who enjoys reading history books. At a certain point in the educational process those who get no enjoyment from reading history should cease to have it required of them.

Waiting for those who find they enjoy reading history is a vast literature. The best place to begin is with histories dealing with a whole period, say the ancient world or the Roman Empire. Some of the very greatest historians, e.g. Herodotus and Gibbon, wrote splendid works of this sort. Once readers have an acquaintance with the overall story of a period, they can begin to fill in the details by reading the biographies of people who lived during that time. The next step, which students of history will find themselves taking as their detailed knowledge of the period accumulates, is to search out surviving letters and memoirs from the age being studied. These documents are the data from which history books are constructed, so readers who famil-iarize themselves with such documents are in a position to form some tentative generalizations of limited scope which their subsequent reading can be used to test. This is one of the important functions of the study of history; from just such humble beginnings a science of history may one day emerge. Another important function is that 'it can, by the study of individuals, seek to combine the merits of drama or epic poetry with the merit of truth' (*1957a*, 18). The fruits of this function are good in themselves, but they are also good as means, because the richer our knowledge of them the wiser our behaviour is apt to be. 'History is valuable in increasing our knowledge of human nature, because it shows how people may be expected to behave in new situations' (*1957a*, 25). An historically enlarged imagination is a much richer source of hypotheses than is a pristine one.

In the course of one's study of history an historical perspective is gradually developed. What is permanent, or at least long lasting, begins to emerge from the welter of detail. Once developed, this perspective renders judgment much sounder than it was before. 'It is a help towards sanity and calm judgment to acquire the habit of seeing contemporary events in their historical setting, and of imagining them as they will appear when they are in the past. Theologians assure us that God sees all time as though it were present; it is not in human power to do this except to a very limited degree, but in so far as we can do it, it is a help towards wisdom and contemplative insight' (*1957a*, 55). On occasion in his writings he recommends that something like this perspective can be achieved by replacing the names of nations or persons who are engaged in a dispute by letters of the alphabet and then considering the merits of their cases without being distracted by the emotion that use of their names engenders. Our emotional involvement in the present is what we must learn to suspend, if we are to come to view contemporary events under the guise of eternity. Reading old newspapers helps one see that the urgent matters of today will very likely appear less compelling next week or next year.

In this essay, as in all his writings on history, he is concerned to show his contempt for what is called 'philosophy of history'; he does not think it is possible to discover 'some formula according to which human events develop' (*1957a*, 15). Hegel, Marx and Spencer have advanced such philosophies of history, but he finds them all fantastic. All of them begin by citing some facts and generalizing upon them, but then the generalizations acquire a life of their own and mere facts are either ignored or tailored to fit. General formulae, he argued, 'can only be made plausible by missing out half the facts' (*1957a*, 15). Such philosophies of history are really mythologies.

A principal theme of this essay, as has already been noted, is the delight which accompanies the reading of history. A good example of the sort of pleasure and profit he found in historical reading is in *Which Way to Peace?* To illustrate what can happen when a belief is held fanatically, he turned to history:

> Fanaticism springs from the pursuit of some one narrow end at the expense of all others. A remarkable example is given in Henry C. Lea's *History of the Inquisition in the Middle Ages*. A small sect grew up in Italy which held the heretical opinion that it is wicked to eat meat. No one would have objected to vegetarianism as a practice, but as an ethical doctrine it came within the purview of the Inquisition. The sect was persecuted and its adherents took refuge in the mountains, from which they made descents as freebooters, since the barren summits afforded no sustenance. At length armed bands surrounded them, and made their marauding expeditions impossible, but they still managed, by night attacks, to kill a certain number of their besiegers. It was only animals that their creed forbade them to eat, as to cannibalism, it was silent. Accordingly they subsisted upon the flesh of their persecutors. At length they were overcome, and their leader, without a groan, endured the most appalling tortures, which were ended at last by his death. (*1936*, 200–1.)

Russell took delight, as most of us do, in examples which approach the absurd, and his delight was compounded when he found them in history books.

In *History as an Art* (1954), his last work on history, he raises at once the old question of whether history is an art or a science, and replies that it is both. It getting its facts straight, and, if possible, discovering causal laws linking limited sets of facts, it is a science, but it takes art to bring these discoveries to the consumer, including, of course, the general reader. This requirement demands that history books be interesting, otherwise their readership will be small. If they are interesting – and by this he means written with feeling without distorting facts – people will read them, and they will be improved by reading them, for they will better understand their place in the scheme of things than they formerly did. 'History makes one aware that there is no finality in human affairs; there is not a static perfection and an unimprovable wisdom to be achieved' (*1961*, 536). Reading history is an antidote to 'cocksure certainty' of which the world has too much at present. If the readership of history books can be increased, there is likely to be an increase of both pleasure and sanity in the world. He acknowledges that people do not read as much now as they used to do, and he finds this regrettable. 'People go to the movies, or listen to the radio, or watch television. They indulge in a curious passion for changing their position on the earth's surface as quickly as possible, which they combine with an attempt to make all parts of the earth's surface look alike' (*1961*, 541). But if they can be induced to read history books they will find such splendid pieces of information as this: 'The Emperor Frederick II, for example, most certainly does not deserve to be imitated, but he makes a splendid piece in one's mental furniture. The Wonder of the World, tramping hither and thither with his menagerie, completed at last by his Prime Minister in a cage, debating Moslem sages, winning crusades in spite of being excommunicate, is a figure that I should be sorry not to know about' (*1961*, 540). Such moments of pleasure made life under the shadow of nuclear warfare more endurable.

On his ninetieth birthday he published *History of the World in Epitome (For Use in Martian Infant Schools)*, a tiny book whose entire text reads: 'Since Adam and Eve ate the apple, man has never refrained from any folly of which he was capable.' Then comes 'The End' opposite a photograph of a mushroom cloud.

XII
THE PROPER ROLE OF EDUCATION
IN THE LIFE OF THE CHILD

Education became an important interest of Russell during the time he was thinking about the political and social causes of the First World War. His principle of growth demands a theory of education which will maximize it. A chapter of *Principles of Social Reconstruction* sketches a version of the theory that is commonly called 'progressive education'. The basic assumption is that the principle of growth which motivates children is on the whole good and that most bad qualities are produced by thwarting a child's impulses and desires in arbitrary ways. It is not his opinion that undisciplined growth will automatically produce good qualities in people, but he does believe that discipline should take account of the direction of growth, encouraging without distorting it, for the direction is much more likely, in very young children at least, to be right than wrong. This theory of education, which has much in common with that of John Dewey, is in sharp contrast to an older view which assumed childish nature to be bad and which could be made good only by rote-learning enforced by corporeal punishment. Progressivists argue that if one permits the child to develop, teaching it self-control when appropriate or required, a better adult will emerge.

This is also Russell's position, but he placed special emphasis on teaching the child to think. His educational method, he liked to argue, would gradually produce a population with a different mental outlook from that then common.

> It is possible that there would not be much independence of thought even if education did everything to promote it; but there would certainly be more than there is at present. If the object were to make pupils think, rather than to make them accept certain conclusions, education would be conducted quite differently: there would be less rapidity of instruction and more discussion, more occasions when pupils are encouraged to express themselves, more attempt to make education concern itself with matters in which the pupils feel some interest. (*1916*, 163–4.)

Much of what he advocated is now widely practised, especially in the early years of schooling.

After the birth of his first two children, John in 1921 and Kate in 1923, he became interested in pre-school education. The book he wrote for parents, *On Education: Especially in Early Childhood* (*Education and the Good Life* in the United States), is, for the most part concerned with education of character during the first six years of life. For his basic assumption about childish nature he turns again to the principle of growth, although he does not use the language of his earlier book. In *On Education* he describes the child as a bundle of instinctive desires, which can easily be driven into evil ways by wrong methods of instruction. 'The new-born infant has reflexes and instincts, but no habits' (*1926*, 70). Children are growing things; their growth, like that of plants and animals, should be treated with loving care. By example and reasoned discussion their growth can be kept to the desired direction. 'Education consists in the cultivation of instincts, not in their suppression' (102). There is need for some external discipline, but the aim should be to reduce the need of it to a minimum by helping children discipline themselves. One should start very early, in the first year of life, developing this internal self-discipline. 'A human ego, like a gas, will always expand unless restrained by external pressure. The object of education, in this respect, is to let the external pressure take the form of habits, ideas, and sympathies in the child's own mind, not of knocks and blows and punishments' (117). Regularity is one important condition of success in forming good habits, and good habits are the essence of self-discipline.

The child's desire for regularity in its daily life is the source, he believes, of a principle which, as we have seen, is basic to his theory of knowledge. 'I have sometimes thought that belief in the uniformity of nature, which is said to be a postulate of science, is entirely derived from the wish for safety. We can cope with the expected, but if the laws of nature were suddenly changed we should perish' (78). Throughout his popular writings one finds remarks of this sort which give to his views a ring of unity that, antecedently at least, seems unlikely, given the great variety in the subject-matter.

His advice on the way instruction in intellectual matters should proceed owes a great deal to his philosophical method. On all factual matters a child's questions should be answered in the same way, be they about the moon or death or sex. That way is to lay out the facts of the matter without suggesting there is any emotional difference involved in the subjects being questioned. Children will pick up any hint of embarrassment and will attach it to a subject to which it is inappropriate. Children have a natural curiosity, and it is easy for the imaginative teacher to fill their need for knowledge in a way that encourages intellectual growth. Given the facts of a case children will theorize about it; when they do, the teacher can, by proceeding sympathetically, teach them the rudiments of criticism. In this way they will learn about rival theories, negative instances, probability, and the importance of suspending or qualifying their judgments. Instruction so carried out will produce adults who have a wish to know the truth and who have developed intellectual habits likely to discover it.

Shortly after publishing *On Education* in 1926 Russell and his second wife, Dora, were faced with the practical question of educating their two children. Believing his own experience of private tuition on the whole to have been bad, largely because it deprived him of companions his own age, they resolved that their children should be sent to school. After looking into all the likely schools, including the most progressive ones, they concluded that none of them were progressive enough, so they decided to establish a school in which they would enrol their own children along with others. Beacon Hill School was duly founded and both Russells taught in it; there were also several other teachers on the staff. A conscious effort was made by all teachers to teach according to the theory Russell had laid out in his book. In practice, however, he found matters did not go as theory predicted. This was partly due to the nature of the children they were went as pupils, many of whom would have tried the patience of a saint. They had been unwise to advertise the school as they did; it attracted, for the most part, problem children whose well-entrenched bad habits were not improved by being thrown together with others of the same ilk. The Russells and their teachers did have considerable success with some of their pupils, but, on the whole, he judged the school a failure.

After he had separated from Dora and left the school in her hands, he published *Education and the Social Order* (*Education and the Modern World* in the United States), in which he attempted to reconcile two conflicting aims of education. On the one hand, the State wants the schools to turn out dependable citizens; on the other hand, the advancement of knowledge requires that the schools develop the best talents of each pupil to the highest degree. Of course it is not only the advancement of knowledge that makes the latter demand; it is also all of those who believe in human potential and think it has not yet been fully realized. The State, however, controls most of the schools, so it is more likely to prevail. His book is aimed at citizens in the hope that if they are sufficiently aroused they will demand the reform of education along the lines he recommends.

The theory of education he advocates is the familiar one. In this book he calls it 'the negative theory of education' and gives as its essence 'that the sole purpose of education is to provide opportunities of growth and to remove hampering influences' (*1939, 29*). Because of the complexity of the society in which we live, he does not hold this theory in its pure form. The theory holds without qualification for the education of the emotions, but only with qualifications for intellectual and technical education. The complexity of the present world requires that students be given positive guidance if they are to survive and prosper. The positive requirement in education must be carefully controlled to avoid lapsing into the discredited educational methods of earlier times. Rote-learning must be used sparingly and then only when no better method is known. Over-education is a real danger, but it can be guarded against by observing certain conditions. Firstly, emotional strain should be reduced to a minimum; this means that ways other than examinations be favoured for measuring progress. Secondly, all instruction serving no purpose should be eliminated; this means that children 'should not learn things merely because they always have been learnt' (175); this rule doubtless reflects his own unhappy experience with the classical languages, which he had to master to a certain level in order to be admitted to Cambridge. Thirdly, in advanced years what should be taught exclusively is the method or methods by which inquiry is conducted; this means that examinations which seek the 'right' answers be abolished. It is readily apparent that the goal of education in this book as in the earlier one is the acquisition of a scientific frame of mind.

If a whole generation could be educated in this way, the problem of the conflict between the individual and the citizen would evaporate, because such a population would reorganize society in a more rational way and eliminate the causes of patriotic feeling which are at the root of present differences between nations. This is unlikely to happen on a wide enough scale to bring about the desired changes. What then can be done? Individuals persuaded by Russell can do their bit by working to free the world of large-scale wars and superstition; they can also bring pressure to bear upon their local school authority to encourage those among its teachers who love teaching and to discourage those who love governing other teachers. Good teachers help their pupils acquire both 'an internal harmony of intelligence, emotion, and will, and an external harmony with the wills of others' (244). A person who enjoys both kinds of harmony is likely to lead a life that is satisfactory both to himself and to others – to be both a good person and a good citizen.

XIII
SOME THOUGHTS ON HIS ACHIEVEMENTS

This brief survey of Russell's work will have given the reader a glimpse of some of his achievements. But it is only a glimpse, and, with regard to his technical work in logic and the foundations of mathematics, it is hardly even that. Technical subjects defy summary in ordinary prose. The reader who has never looked into *Principia Mathematica* will realize the truth of this upon examining that book. Nor has there been space to give more than examples of his philosophical work. His philosophical writings fill many volumes, and some of the problems he tackles in them are far removed from ordinary experience; and then, of course, he has a tendency to return to the same problem and have another go at solving it, often with a fresh terminology. Again a summary would have to be very long, if it attempted to convey the subtlety of his thought.

Russell's most important achievement, which he shares with Whitehead, is the writing of *Principia Mathematica*. Building on the work of many others they created the science of mathematical logic. In the course of his work on this big book, Russell made many important, and enduring, contributions to logic and the foundations of mathematics. His theory of descriptions was outlined in Chapter IV; the technique it intro-

duces for symbolizing statements involving definite
descriptions is now a standard part of any textbook in
symbolic logic. There has been less agreement about
the philosophical aspects of the theory, which were first
questioned by P. F. Strawson in 1950 in 'On Referring'.
Since that time a vast literature has accumulated, itself
a testimony to the great importance of the problem
which Russell was the first to take seriously.

The theory of descriptions is just one example of his
work in logic; another is the logic of relations. The
logic of relations is the logic of predicates requiring
more than one name for their expression: 'Earl is
married to Evelyn', 'Clinton is sitting between Major
and Kohl', and 'Ronnie bought a vase for Roberta to
give to Tammy' are examples of relational statements.
As children all of us learn many logical relations which
hold between relational statements. Examples (with
letters replacing names) are: 'if x is married to y, then y
is married to x'; 'if x is the son of y, then y is either the
mother or the father of x'; and 'if x is the second cousin
of y, then x is a grandchild of w and y is a grandchild of
z and w and z are siblings'. After he had learned
Peano's symbolic notation Russell extended it to the
logic of relations and developed that logic in a
systematic way. He was helped here, as he was in all of
his work in logic, by the work of his predecessors in the
nineteenth century.

The logic of relations gave him some new analytical
tools which he put to immediate use in philosophy.
Many earlier philosophers had assumed there were only
one-place predicates, such as 'x is pink' or 'x is a
butterfly', and that those predicates which appeared to
require more than one name for their expression, such
as 'x is married to y', could be analyzed into two

subject-predicate statements, one attributing a property to x and the other attributing a property to y. These philosophers argued that if it is true that x is married to y, then both x and y, individually, must have some property they would not have if they were not married to one another. Using examples such as this one, which lends their argument a certain plausibility, they concluded, negatively, that there are no external relations, and, positively, that all relations are internal to their subjects. This line of thinking, when carried to its limit, leads to a monistic metaphysics, and to the view, ultimately, that there is one and only one entity which serves as subject in every proposition. F. H. Bradley is an important British philosopher who held this position.

Russell attacked the monist's position as inconsistent with the logic of relations. Take any relation R of which it is true to say that if x bears the relation R to y, then y does not bear the relation R to x. Such relations are very common; consider, for instance, 'x is taller than y'. Everyone recognizes the truth of the statement, 'if Jack is taller than Ann, then Ann is not taller than Jack'. Now the argument for internal relations requires the production of two statements which together exhaust the meaning of 'x is taller than y'. The natural way to try to carry out this programme is to assign numerical values to the heights of both x and y, say, 'x is six feet tall' and 'y is five feet tall'. So far, it seems, so good. But we have not yet exhausted the meaning of the original statement. We require, Russell pointed out, another statement, such as 'six feet is taller than five feet', but this statement reintroduces the very relation, 'is taller than', that we were trying to analyze away. There is, he concluded, no way of carrying out the monist's programme without admitting at least one relational statement, so the programme is doomed to failure. Some relational statements must be admitted, so there is more than one thing in the world. Hence pluralism is true. Russell's own metaphysics, of which a sample has been given in Chapter V, is self-consciously pluralistic.

His discovery of the paradox that bears his name has had far-ranging consequences. The reader will recall from Chapter II how easily his paradox emerges from common sense. The reasoning involved is such as to appeal to untutored intuition; and the principle of extensionality, an important premiss in his argument, seems intuitively self-evident. But the conclusion reached is repugnant to that same intuition. Clearly intuition is not a completely reliable guide in logic. Since the discovery of his paradox logicians have been at pains to examine every argument they study in full detail. Every suppressed premiss must be stated; every step in the proof must be made explicit; and the whole analysis must be made available for public scrutiny. Only by these means can one ensure that no fatal defect has been overlooked. Intuition can still serve as a guide in logic, and in that role it is indispensable, but the steps it suggests must still be independently verified before they can be taken as correct. Russell discusses at length the roles of intuition and logic in acquiring knowledge in his essay, 'Mysticism and Logic'.

This legacy of full and detailed disclosure, which Russell and the other pioneers in symbolic logic bequeathed to their successors, helped prepare the way for the design of the digital computer. This computer is essentially a logic machine, which, when given detailed instructions and some data as input, will carry out the calculations required quickly and accurately. Since such a machine is devoid of intuition, every step of the calculation to be performed must be laid out and the input data must be explicitly rendered in machine language. In ordinary life we tend to skip steps in reasoning (because they are obvious) and to omit stating some of our premisses (because they are articles of common sense). In daily life such shortcuts seldom cause trouble. It took Russell's genius to show that the habits of daily life led to contradiction. The lesson he learned in such a hard way is now learned by many very young children. In their interactions with computers they soon discover that the omission of any required step, however trivial it may seem to their intuition, must be executed, if the computer is to perform the assigned task.

It will be clear from these examples that his work in logic has had a profound and permanent effect on the way that subject has developed since the publication of *Principia Mathematica*. The credit, of course, is not all his, and he would be the first to acknowledge that fact. The development of symbolic logic was a cooperative enterprise, with many distinguished contributors; Russell and Whitehead just happened to come along when the subject was ripe for systematization. In the course of their work they broke a lot of new ground, especially on the philosophical side, the part of their work for which Russell was principally responsible. But even though he was responsible for the philosophical aspects of their work, it remains true that there is hardly a line of the book of which he is the sole author. In *My Philosophical Development* (1959) he has two chapters on the writing of *Principia Mathematica*; it is the best source for gaining an acquaintance with the division of labour which went into that great work.

In philosophy his most enduring contribution to date has been the championship of the analytical method. Again he was not solely responsible; G. E. Moore was equally involved in the development of this way of doing philosophy. The revolution they effected has been profound and sweeping. Analytical philosophy is dominant everywhere in the English-speaking world, and the analytical method is applied in every branch of philosophy, from aesthetics to metaphysics. Discussions of questions of logic and meaning are as apt to turn up in a paper in the philosophy of religion as they are in an essay in the philosophy of science. Students of philosophy must learn logic if for no other reason than to prepare themselves to read the current literature in their field.

The spread of the analytical method has transformed philosophy in a number of important ways. There is, in the first place, the use of a wide variety of techniques to lay bare the logic of the matter being studied. Use of these techniques tends to accentuate the intellectual aspects of a problem and to attenuate the emotional aspects, if there are any, associated with the matter to hand. Analytical philosophers attempt to state an argument fully (using the notation of symbolic logic if it helps to reveal the argument's structure) in order to determine whether or not the argument is a good one. In the second place, most analytical philosophers think of their work as contributing to a cooperative enterprise. They expect other philosophers to read their writings critically and to make use of any of their results which further their own work. Philosophy, in the English-speaking world at least, has become a much more co-operative venture than it was when Russell and Moore were young. Journals have multiplied to keep pace with the level of research activity, but, for some groups, even journal publication is too slow; they prefer to circulate photocopies, or now electronic copies, of their work in progress to a select group of fellow workers in order to benefit from their criticism without undue delay. Finally, analytical philosophers tend to think of themselves as more akin to mathematicians and scientists than to artists and literary people. Like Russell such philosophers think of themselves as discovering truths and as contributing to the development of a science. There is a tendency for philosophical papers to resemble more closely scientific papers in their structure and writing than literary essays. Although this is the direction Russell urged philosophers to take, it is unlikely, given his concern with style, that he himself would be comfortable with the new standard of writing that has evolved. He would, however, be happy with the more scientific attitude which has produced that standard.

It is undeniable that Russell has had a profound effect on the way philosophy is done, but what of his own philosophical contributions? How well have they fared? To this question it is impossible to give a very definite answer. He always claimed that the positions he defended were merely the best hypotheses available, given the present evidence, and he urged his fellow philosophers to regard his work as tentative and very probably in need of correction. As use of the analytical method spread, philosophers tended to take him at his word. They examined his proposed solutions to problems carefully, using the latest logical tools, and they frequently found his positions wanting, at least in part. When one of his results survived examination, it often became the starting-point for further work. His own work, then, has figured in two ways in subsequent philosophical writing: it has at times been shown to be deficient in one way or other, and thus has functioned to warn of a blind alley and to spur others to attempt to find a better answer to the question; and it has sometimes proved to be the best hypothesis available, and thus served as the foundation for further development. Russell, on occasion, contended that really good work simply becomes part of its subject and ceases to be regarded as the position of its discoverer. To a certain extent some of his work in logic measures up to this standard; it is repeated in every logic textbook, usually now without attribution.

When we pass from the technical areas of his work to the more popular parts, assessment is much less easy. For a very long time he was a focus for many causes, some of which were successful, at least in part. Many of the ideas he advanced, whether original with him or not, concerning education and the relations between the sexes, are now taken for granted. At the time he was championing them they were denounced by many as the very epitome of evil. Companionate marriage, which he recommended in *Marriage and Morals* in 1929, will serve as an example. Now very respectable people live together without benefit of marriage vows. How much of the credit for this change is due his book it is impossible to say; but it is likely that it had some effect, because it was widely read by the young, and, perhaps more importantly, denounced by earnest moralists. The denunciations frequently had the opposite effect from the one intended; their outcries brought the book to the attention of potential readers who until then had not heard of it. When all is said and done, it is likely that Russell left the world a different and, from his point of view, better place than he found it, especially as regards interpersonal relations.

In both religion and politics his views proved to run in the same direction the Western democracies were evolving. Opposed to organized religion for nearly all of his life, he was concerned to decrease the power of the Church whenever an opportunity to do so presented itself. Many others shared his position, and gradually their power began to be felt. A much more secular society has emerged during the last ninety years than the young Russell and other freethinkers at the turn of the century would have dreamed possible. In politics he was essentially a liberal democrat, and, again, despite many dark hours, the Western democracies have remained liberal and democratic. It is of their essence that they both accord individual citizens a large measure of liberty and also encourage them to partic-ipate, to a certain limited extent at least, in policy decisions. Such a milieu suited Russell to a tee, because he nearly always had something he wanted to say on important public concerns. and he did so, often and vigorously. Such participation helps to keep democracy alive, for it tends to foster in the young a sense that it is their duty to participate in political affairs. His writings and his political activities had this salutary effect on many in the younger generations.

On the large question of nuclear warfare judgment again is difficult. He certainly did bring the matter forcibly to the attention of many people, and he induced many of these same people to work – and some of them to work very hard – to lessen the chance of nuclear war. Many thousands marched and participated in sit-downs. But for a long time there was not much change in the policies of the states with nuclear arsenals. Then suddenly in 1989 the Cold War ended, leaving a very messy set of nuclear problems behind. Had he been alive one feels sure he would have welcomed the end of hostilities and would have turned his energies to ridding the world of its nuclear residue. The reformer's work, as he so well knew, is never done.

There is a complaint made against Russell which requires discussion, because it has a bearing upon the worth accorded his philosophical work. His fellow philosophers have often criticized him for changing his mind on important philosophical matters during the course of his long career. To cite a well-known instance: C. D. Broad, who had been Russell's student at Cambridge, commented in 1924: 'As we all know, Mr Russell produces a different system of philosophy every few years, and Dr Moore never produces one at all. "*Si Russell savait, si Moore pouvait*" seems the only adequate comment on the situation; but I owe more that I can tell to the speculative boldness of the one and the meticulous accuracy of the other' (Muirhead *1924*, I: 79). Broad was not, of course, accusing Russell of inconsistency, because he did not claim that Russell held both his old and his new positions at the same time. There is after all a difference between development and inconsistency. But Broad does seem to be suggesting that a philosopher should not change his mind, and others have said so explicitly. Oddly enough, the same criticism does not seem to be leveled at Wittgenstein, who also produced at least two systems of philosophy. Russell did cast aside former positions in favour of what he took to be better ones, although the differences between the two are often, when examined closely, not very great. Charges that he had abandoned earlier doctrines did not trouble him, because, before giving up a position he had convinced himself that it was deficient in some way. Scientists behaved this way towards their subject-matter, and his method bid him emulate them. Indeed, it is just because his philosophical work was driven by method that his output has the overall appearance that it has.

To place Russell in the philosophical spectrum, let us outline two extreme positions. The work of the first group of philosophers is determined by the conclusions they wish to establish – the 'here are the conclusions on which I base my premisses' school. In 'Mysticism and Logic' Russell points to Parmenides and his school as an almost pure example of this way of doing philosophy. Through mystical insight, or intuition, Parmenides was convinced that what was real was static, and he used his considerable logical ability to find arguments to support this view. Two axioms, 'what is, is' and 'what is not, is not', were advanced to prove that there was no change, no plurality, and so on, through a long list of negatives. His disciple, Zeno the Eliatic, invented paradoxes, of which Achilles and the tortoise is perhaps the best known, to show that, appearances to the contrary notwithstanding, motion was unreal. These are only some of the startling doctrines that this school defended. Once the principal tenets of the school had been 'proved' there was no where to go, so the school tended to become an historical oddity, but not before it greatly influenced Plato.

At the other end of the spectrum are the philosophers who adopt a specific method and use it to arrive at positions on all of the philosophical questions with which they attempt to deal. Amongst them the most extreme are those who adopt a method which requires no check with experience as the system is developed. When Russell writes of Hegel and Marx he accuses them of this type of mistake. Following their method – a three-step logic – wherever it leads, they are led into what seem gross absurdities judged from his point of view. Any method without provision for periodic checks with experience to determine whether modifications are required will result, sooner or later, in disastrous conclusions. Russell's most influential teachers at Cambridge held positions of this sort, leading them to defend such conclusions as 'time is unreal' and 'there is only one subject'. G. E. Moore, with whom Russell was closely associated at this time, used to ridicule these conclusions, by such means as tossing two peas in his hand and demanding to know whether his listener (who was an Hegelian) denied that he had two peas in his hand. Most of them did deny it by using the distinction between appearance and reality: apparently there are two peas but in reality there is only one thing, and then embarking upon a long argument in support of their claim. But they failed to convince Moore and Russell that they were right.

In between these two extremes all sorts of mixtures are possible, and the work of most philosophers embodies some of both approaches. Russell, as will be clear from what has been said, favoured unity of method rather than unity of results. When he was a student he was persuaded by his Hegelian teachers that method, and not some set of desired conclusions, was the correct starting point in philosophy. But, after attempting to apply their method for several years, he came to the conclusion that it was fundamentally defective. So he abandoned the dialectic and 'since then', he told Lady Ottoline in a letter of 28 September 1911, 'I have had only developments, no revolutions'. Later in the same letter he remarked: 'Since then I have only hoped that philosophy could show that we do know something; and to find out whether this is so has been my main business.' Philosophy was to be treated as one of the sciences, albeit un underdeveloped one, instead of the search for a creed. In effect he returned to what he had learned from studying the writings of John Stuart Mill, his godfather, before he went up to Cambridge; that study had given him a healthy respect for the role of experience in human knowledge, even though he thought Mill had overplayed the role of experience in mathematics. Whatever method he adopted for his philosophical work would have to allow for appeals to experience. Surprisingly, his work on the foundations of mathematics reinforced his respect for empiricism. In logical analysis one began by collecting together all the puzzling statements of a certain sort that required an explanation, these were clearly analogous to the unexplained facts with which a scientist begins his enquiry, the effort to find explanatory hypotheses in the two cases and the manner in which they are tested for adequacy once found, were also similar. Reflection on these similarities led him to formulate his 'scientific method in philosophy'. For the rest of his career he used this method whenever he dealt with philosophical problems. His work is unified by his method. To this extent he agreed with his Hegelian teachers.

By its very nature the analytical method, as it is now usually called, yields different results as the initial input changes. When Russell returned to a philosophical problem after a period of years away from it, he had, not only his past experience to draw upon, but also whatever new information had accumulated in the interval. Others may have criticized his earlier tentative results, and he has to take any of their criticisms which withstand his logical scrutiny into account; still others may have published tentative solutions to the problem, and he must examine these with an eye to the light they may cast on the problem as he now understands it. Thus the initial conditions the second time around will never be the same, so the outcome will not be the same. In Russell's opinion, simply to adopt a position and forever after defend it would have been to abandon the scientific method, and, hence, the search for truth.

His method, it must be said, suited to perfection another of his mental strengths. Broad hits upon it when he praises Russell's 'speculative boldness'. Russell did love to speculate. His writings are full of provocative propositions, some of which he argues for at length, and others which he throws out just because they are worth the reader's consideration. When he speculates freely, he tells his reader that he does not know whether what he is saying is true, and that it should not, therefore, be accepted as true without further inquiry. His method demands that he give that warning. Provocative speculations are intended to spur thought, and encouraging thought was, for him, almost a sacred duty. In *Principles of Social Reconstruction*, written during war-time, there is a soaring passage on the importance of thought:

> Men fear thought as they fear nothing else on earth – more than ruin, more even than death. Thought is subversive and revolutionary, destructive and terrible; thought is

merciless to privilege, established institutions, and comfortable habits; thought is anarchic and lawless, indifferent to authority, careless of the well-tried wisdom of the ages. Thought looks into the pit of hell and is not afraid. It sees man, a feeble speck, surrounded by unfathomable depths of silence; yet it bears itself proudly, as unmoved as if it were lord of the universe. Thought is great and swift and free, the light of the world, and the chief glory of man. (178–9.)

Moore, one feels sure, could never have written such a passage; it fails of 'the meticulous accuracy' which Broad attributes, rightly as it seems to me, to Moore. In one of his letters to Lady Ottoline Russell remarked: 'I don't think tame well-behaved people ever know anything of the mad fire just below the smooth surface of life. But whether it is worth while to know of it, I don't know' (#886).

Usually calling this mad fire 'passion', Russell credits it with his most important intellectual accomplishments. On 30 April 1912 he told Lady Ottoline something of what he put into *Principia Mathematica*:

It is not an easy thing to move the world. I have put into the world a great body of abstract thought, which is moving those whom one might hope to move by it, and will ultimately, probably, move many people who will have never heard of philosophy. What makes it vital, what makes it fruitful, is the absolute unbridled Titanic passion that I have put into it. It is passion that has made my intellect clear, passion that has made me never stop to ask myself if the work was worth doing, passion that has made me not care if no human being ever read a word of it; it is passion that enables me to sit for years before a blank page, thinking the whole time about one probably trivial point which I could not get right. That same passion now has gone into my other writing. (#429.)

In a letter a few days earlier he remarked that 'philosophy is a reluctant mistress – one can only reach her heart with the cold steel in the hand of passion' (#423). Passion is clearly the driving force behind getting the work done, and, although the effort itself does not appear in the work, still some of the passion remains and gives the finished work its beauty. Philosophy, in contrast to philosophizing, may be likened to a building after the architect and builders have departed; the passion that remains fixed in the completed structure is perhaps only a small fraction of the total expended, but it accounts for a great deal of the structure's value, including its beauty. 'What people really enjoy in writing or music is just the last drop of anguish in the man's soul: they take the place of gladiatorial shows' (#429).

It is plain, I think, that only a method, and not a set of conclusions, could have driven Russell. He was simply too vital a thinker to have adopted a position early in life and spent the rest of his life refining and defending it. In a letter to Lady Ottoline of 28 September 1911 he spoke directly to this matter:

> A scheme which I have for philosophical work is this: there have always been rival theories in philospohy on numbers of questions, and it has been thought necessary for a philosopher to choose a side, as if it were politics, and swear that his side can be proved right and the other wrong. In many of these perennial controversies, I believe there is not and never can be a jot of evidence for either side, but that by a further effort of abstraction one can arrive at something which both sides have in common, and which can be accepted as fairly certain. What is wanted for this is the particular kind of logical instrument which Whitehead and I have perfected. (#198.)

What would we have thought of him had he taken the course he here repudiates? No doubt he would have been labeled and set aside in the way, say, his contemporary, Bernard Bosanquet, has been, to be dusted off occasionally when a specimen of that sort is wanted. Instead, Russell elected to stir the philosophical pot, and many a less adventurous thinker has been grateful to him for it. For him the world was not neat and tidy like a fussy governess's nursery, but a blooming, buzzing confusion, which presented the philosopher with all sorts of delightful and interesting problems. Some order could be introduced into the world through careful and sustained thinking, using a method which took the relevant facts into account, but there would always remain enough unsolved puzzles to gladden the heart of any young philosopher.

BIBLIOGRAPHY OF WORKS
CITED OR MENTIONED

Works by Bertrand Russell

1896   *German Social Democracy.*
        London: Longmans, Green.

1897   *An Essay on the Foundations of Geometry.*
        Cambridge: At the University Press.

1900   *A Critical Exposition of the Philosophy of*
        Leibniz.
        Cambridge: At the University Press.

1903   *The Principles of Mathematics.*
        Cambridge: At the University Press.

1909   'The Elements of Ethics'.
        Reprinted in his *1992.*

1910   *Anti-Suffragist Anxieties.*
        London: The People's Suffrage Federation.
        Reprinted in his *1985.*

1910   *Philosophical Essays.*
        London: Longmans, Green.

1910–13 *Principia Mathematica.*
        With Alfred North Whitehead. 3 vols.
        Cambridge: At the University Press. Second
        edition, 1925.

1912   *The Problems of Philosophy.*
          London: Williams and Norgate; New York:
          Henry Holt and Company.

1914   *Our Knowledge of the External World as a*
          Field for Scientific Method in Philosophy.
          Chicago and London: The Open Court
          Publishing Company.

1916   *Justice in War-Time.* Chicago and London:
          The Open Court Publishing Company.

1916   *Principles of Social Reconstruction.*
          London: George Allen & Unwin: New
          York: The Century Company, as *Why Men*
          Fight: A Method of Abolishing the
          International Duel.

1917   *Political Ideals.*
          New York: The Century Company.

1918   *Mysticism and Logic and Other Essays.*
          London and New York: Longmans, Green.

1918a   *Roads to Freedom: Socialism, Anarchism,*
          and Syndicalism.
          London: George Allen & Unwin; New
          York: Henry Holt, as *Proposed Roads to*
          Freedom: Socialism, Anarchism, and
          Syndicalism.

1918b   'The German Peace Offer'.
          The Tribunal. 3 January 1918. Reprinted in
          his *1968*.

1919   *Introduction to Mathematical Philosophy.*
          London: George Allen & Unwin; New
          York: The Macmillan Company.

1920   *The Practice and Theory of Bolshevism.*
London: George Allen & Unwin; New
York: Harcourt, Brace and Howe, as
Bolshevism: Practice and Theory.

1921   *The Analysis of Mind.*
London: George Allen & Unwin; New
York: The Macmillan Company.

1922   *The Problem of China.*
London: George Allen & Unwin; New
York: The Century Company.

1923   *The ABC of Atoms.*
London: Kegan Paul, Trench, Trubner; New
York: E.P. Dutton.

1925   *The ABC of Relativity.*
London: Kegan Paul, Trench, Trubner; New
York: Harper & Brothers.

1925   *What I Believe.*
London: Kegan Paul, Trench, Trubner; New
York: E.P. Dutton.

1926   *On Education, Especially in Early
Childhood.*
London: George Allen & Unwin; New
York: Boni & Liveright, as *Education and
the Good Life.*

1927   *The Analysis of Matter.*
London: Kegan Paul, Trench, Trubner; New
York: Harcourt, Brace.

1927a   *An Outline of Philosophy.*
London: George Allen & Unwin; New
York: W.W. Norton, as *Philosophy.*

1927b   *Why I Am Not a Christian.*
London: Watts; New York: The Truth
Seeker Company.

1929   *Marriage and Morals.*
London: George Allen & Unwin; New
York: Horace Liveright.

1930   *The Conquest of Happiness.*
London: George Allen & Unwin; New
York: Horace Liveright.

1931   *The Scientific Outlook.*
London: George Allen & Unwin; New
York: W. W. Norton.

1932   *Education and the Social Order.*
London: George Allen & Unwin; New
York: W. W. Norton, as *Education and the
Modern World.*

1934   *Freedom and Organization, 1814–1914.*
London: George Allen & Unwin; New
York: W. W. Norton, as *Freedom versus
Organization, 1814-1914.*

1935   *Religion and Science.*
London: Thornton Butterworth; New York:
Henry Holt.

1936   *Which Way to Peace?*
London: Michael Joseph.

1938   *Power: A New Social Analysis.*
London: George Allen & Unwin; New
York: W. W. Norton.

1940   *An Inquiry into Meaning and Truth.*
London: George Allen & Unwin; New
York: W. W. Norton.

1943   *How to Read and Understand History: The
        Past as the Key to the Future.*
        Girard, Kansas: Haldeman-Julius
        Publications. Reprinted in his *1957a.*

1945   *A History of Western Philosophy, and Its
        Connection with Political and Social
        Circumstances from the Earliest Times to
        the Present Day.*
        New York: Simon and Schuster; London:
        George Allen & Unwin, 1946.

1947   *Philosophy and Politics.*
        London: Published for the National Book
        League by The Cambridge University Press.

1948   *Human Knowledge: Its Scope and Limits.*
        London: George Allen & Unwin; New
        York: Simon and Schuster.

1949   *Authority and the Individual.*
        London: George Allen & Unwin; New
        York: Simon and Schuster.

1950   *Unpopular Essays.*
        London: George Allen & Unwin; New
        York: Simon and Schuster.

1951   *New Hopes for a Changing World.*
        London: George Allen & Unwin; New
        York: Simon and Schuster.

1952   *The Impact of Science on Society.*
        London: George Allen & Unwin; New
        York: Simon and Schuster.

1954   *Human Society in Ethics and Politics.*
        London: George Allen & Unwin; New
        York: Simon and Schuster.

1954   *History As an Art.*
          Aldington, Ashford, Kent: The Hand and
          Flower Press. Reprinted in his *1961*.

1956   *Logic and Knowledge: Essays, 1901–1950.*
          Edited by Robert Charles Marsh. London:
          George Allen & Unwin; New York: The
          Macmillan Company.

1956a   *Portraits from Memory and Other Essays.*
          London: George Allen & Unwin; New
          York: Simon and Schuster.

1957   *Why I Am Not a Christian and Other
          Essays on Religion and Related Subjects.*
          Edited with an appendix on the *Bertrand
          Russell Case* by Paul Edwards. London:
          George Allen & Unwin; New York: Simon
          and Schuster.

1957a   *Understanding History and Other Essays.*
          New York: Philosophical Library.

1959   *My Philosophical Development.*
          London: George Allen & Unwin; New
          York: Simon and Schuster.

1961   *The Basic Writings of Bertrand Russell,
          1903–1959.*
          Edited by Robert E. Egner and Lester E.
          Denonn. London: George Allen & Unwin;
          New York: Simon and Schuster.

1962   *History of the World in Epitome (For Use
          in Martian Infant Schools).*
          London: Gaberbocchus. Reprinted in his
          1972.

1963 *Unarmed Victory.*
London: George Allen & Unwin and
Penguin Books; New York: Simon and
Schuster.

1967 *War Crimes in Vietnam.*
London: George Allen & Unwin; New
York: Monthly Review Press.

1967 *The Autobiography of Bertrand Russell.* I
Volume 1. London: George Allen & Unwin;
Boston and Toronto: Little Brown and
Company, 1967a.

1968 *The Autobiography of Bertrand Russell.*
Volume 2. London: George Allen & Unwin;
Boston and Toronto: Little Brown and
Company.

1969 *The Autobiography of Bertrand Russell.*
Volume 3. London: George Allen & Unwin;
New York: Simon and Schuster.

1972 *The Collected Stories of Bertrand Russell.*
Compiled and edited by Barry Feinberg.
London: George Allen & Unwin; New
York: Simon and Schuster.

1983 *Cambridge Essays, 1888-99.* London,
Boston, Sydney: George Allen & Unwin.
(The Collected Papers of Bertrand Russell,
Volume 1.)

1984 *Theory of Knowledge: The 1913
Manuscript.*
London, Boston, Sydney: George Allen &
Unwin. (The Collected Papers of Bertrand
Russell, Volume 7.)

1985   *Contemplation and Action, 1902–14.*
       London, Boston, Sydney: George Allen &
       Unwin. (The Collected Papers of Bertrand
       Russell, Volume 12).

1992   *Logical and Philosophical Papers, 1909–13.*
       London and New York: Routledge. (The
       Collected Papers of Bertrand Russell,
       Volume 6.)

Works by Others

CHRISTIE, AGATHA, 1934. *Murder on the Orient
    Express.* London: The Crime Club.

MARX, KARL, 1867–94. *Capital.* Translated by S.
    Moore, E. Aveling and E. Untermann. 3 vols.
    Chicago: Kerr. First edition in German,
    1867–94.

MARX, KARL, AND FRIEDRICH ENGELS, 1888.
    Manifesto of the Communist Party. Authorized
    English translation. London: William Reeves.
    First edition in German, 1848.

MOORE, G.E., 1903. *Principia Ethica.* Cambridge:
    At the University Press.

MUIRHEAD, J.H., ED., 1924. *Contemporary British
    Philosophy: Personal Statements.* (First Series.)
    London: George Allen & Unwin; New York:
    Macmillan.

SANTAYANA, GEORGE, 1913. *Winds of Doctrine:
    Studies in Contemporary Opinion.* New York:

Charles Scribner's Sons; London J. M. Dent & Sons.

STRAWSON, P. F., 1950, 'On Referring'. *Mind: A Quarterly Review of Psychology and Philosophy*. Vol. 59.

WHITEHEAD, ALFRED NORTH, 1898. *A Treatise on Universal Algebra, with Applications*. Cambridge: At the University Press.